Rachel's Tears
&
Mary's Song

John O'Brien

Pen Press Publishers Ltd

First published in Great Britain by
Pen Press Publishers Ltd
39-41, North Road
Islington
London N7 9DP

ISBN 1-905203-72-1

Printed and bound in the UK

A catalogue record of this book is available from
the British Library

Cover painting *'Strong to Save'* by Ellen Barrett

For Phyllis Edwards,
who wept Rachel's tears

*

To Shaun Edwards
a good friend

Acknowledgements

This book began with the suggestion by Father Ulic Troy who asked me to use my writing to help those going through turmoil and needed healing. Afterwards it was felt that the work could apply to anyone with emotional difficulties and pain and who sought consolation.

Many people helped in the realisation of this project and I would like to thank them all. Jacqueline Corkish who helped with the proof reading, Teresa Hand-Campbell who did the typing and a special thanks to Jim and Sheila Harkins, Mike and Mary Ganly, John Ronaghan, Micheál and Roseanne MacManus, Máirtín O'Conner and Mary Concannon, Stephanie Pastoris and my brothers in the Franciscan Order.

I would also like to thank Ellen Barrett who painted the cover for this book.

Michael Drum
Book. Passage & Paths

Contents

Epigraph:

Following the example of our most blessed father Francis, I was seeking this peace with panting spirit – I, a sinner and utterly unworthy, who after our blessed father's death, had become the seventh Minister General of the Friars. It happened that about the time of the thirty-third anniversary of the Saint's death, under divine impulse, I withdrew to Mount La Verna, seeking a place of quiet and desiring to find there peace of spirit. While I was there reflecting on various ways by which the soul ascends into God, there came to mind, among other things, the miracle which had occurred to blessed Francis in this very place, the vision of a winged Seraph in the form of the Crucified. While reflecting on this, I saw that this vision represented our father's rapture in contemplation and the road by which this rapture is reached.

The six wings of the Seraph can rightly be taken to symbolise the six levels of illumination by which, as if by steps or stages, the soul can pass over to peace through ecstatic elevations of Christian wisdom. There is no other path but through the burning love of the Crucified, a love which so transformed Paul into Christ when he was carried up to the third heaven. (2 Cor. 12:2) that he could say: With Christ I am nailed to the cross. I live, now not I, but Christ lives in me. (Gal. 2:20). This love also so absorbed the soul of Francis that his spirit shone through his flesh when for two years before his death he carried in his body the sacred stigmata.

(The Soul's Journey into God, 1:2,3)

There is a loneliness in us that hears. When the soul parts from the company of the ego and its retinue of petty conceits; when we cease to exploit all things but instead pray the world's cry, the world's sigh, our loneliness may hear the living grace beyond all power.

*(**Rabbi Heschel, God In Search of Man**)*

CHAPTER 1: Rachel Weeps for her Children

Prayer has different seasons, the seasons of the heart. As Qoheleth reminds us:

'... There is a season for everything, a time for every occupation under heaven:

A time for giving birth,
a time for dying;
a time for planting,
a time for uprooting what has been planted.
A time for killing,
a time for healing;
a time for knocking down,
a time for building.
A time for tears,
a time for laughter;
a time for mourning,
a time for dancing.
A time for throwing stones away,
a time for gathering them up;
a time for embracing,
a time to refrain from embracing.
A time for searching,
a time for losing;
 a time for keeping,
a time for throwing away.
A time for tearing,

a time for sewing;
a time for keeping silent,
a time for speaking.
A time for loving,
a time for hating;
a time for war.'

(Ecc 3:1-8)

Our prayer can reflect the different seasons of the heart. When the psalmist cries, *"Let everything that breathes praise God"* (Ps150:6) we hear the summer voice of prayer.

It is the voice of Christmas, Easter and Pentecost. The summer voice of prayer is the glad response to the Gospel and it is a vital part of faith and life.

However, there were many times in my life that Ps150 seemed very remote from my experience. It was a season, a time of confusion and deep depression. It is then I turn to the winter voice of prayer, "Out of the depths I cry to You, O God" (Ps 130:1). The winter voice of prayer is the voice of Israel in bondage, wandering in the wilderness and living in exile. It is the voice of Hager, Hannah, Rachel, Jeremiah and Job. It is the voice of Jesus in Gethsemane and on the cross. Like the Easter voice of prayer, the Good Friday voice of prayer belongs to the biblical drama of salvation and to the life and worship of the church. The summer and winter voices of prayer cannot be separated without damage to the life of faith. The risen Jesus bears the wounds of crucifixion. We too must pass through our personal Gethsemane and crosses before transformation and new life.

Rachel's Lament:

Rachel is remembered above all for her lamentations. In one of the most poignant passages of scripture, the prophet Jeremiah describes her inconsolable grief because of the death of her children and the loss of those taken in exile. "A voice is heard in Ramah, lamentation and bitter weeping. Rachel is weeping for her children: she refuses to be comforted for her children, because they are no more..." (Jer 31:15). Rachel refuses any fake consolation. She does not remain silent when facing the loss of her children. She weeps and laments. Her weeping is bitter.

She will not be reconciled to the injustice and violence of the world.

She weeps for herself and anguishes over her loss.

Her children are gone and she weeps because she can no longer see them, hear their laughter or comfort their tears. All that might have been is no longer possible.

There is anger and resistance in Rachel's cry. Rachel's refusal of comfort reflects not only her own anguish but her rage at the senseless slaughter of children. Rachel cries out on behalf of her dead children. She remembers their suffering and she resists consolation while such outrages continue. Her prayer is disconcerting for me and for many other friars. Anger is something I was trained to turn aside from. Any outrage or anger was soothed by 'pious platitudes' and insincere words. Rachel and her prayer invoke facing negative feelings and living through the season of lament.

Rachel laments before God. She pours out her distress to the One who appears to be absent. Then we hear the voice of Yahweh answer Rachel:

"Yahweh says this:

Stop your weeping,
Dry your eyes.
Your hardships will be redressed.
They will come back from the enemy country.
There is hope for your descendants."

(Jer 31: 16-17)

From her lament springs hope. Justice and peace will reign on earth. The prophet Jeremiah, and later Jewish tradition, understands Rachel's tears and lament as expressions of faithfulness.

Her lament is both a protest to and a waiting on God. In her own way, Rachel holds open the possibility of again praising the God of justice and new life.

The story of Rachel, however, has never been as influential in the life and worship of the Christian church. She remains, along with the tradition of lament, an outsider to Christian spirituality. Like Job she is a resister, a protester who refuses the facile consolation of so much spirituality. Most Christians are certainly not inclined to think of Rachel or Job when they look for models of prayer and piety.

I, and many men, were trained not to trust emotion and certainly not negative emotions. To admit to emotion was considered a sign of weakness. Vulnerability was not to be shown. In the lives of many male religious this has had disastrous consequences. In the void caused by denying emotions, depression, alcoholism and other addictions came in. Hegel saw the necessity of integrating emotional intelligence into our lives. He spoke of listening to the voice of emotion and also intellect with reason being the mediator between the two. Freud showed the danger of repression and suppression. Rachel's cry preceded these voices.

Mary's Song of Hope:

Rachel and the cries of lament have largely been placed in the fringes of church life. The Church has been more inclined to look at another biblical woman as a model of prayer, Mary, the Mother of Jesus. Many find their example of prayer in Mary's response to God's call: "Let it be done to me according to Your word" (Lk 1:38).

The contrast seems stark: Rachel refuses, Mary accepts; Rachel weeps, Mary rejoices; Rachel loses her children, Mary is given a child; Rachel expresses rage, Mary is serene.

The truth is never, never as neat and as compact as all that. Rachel's lament paradoxically makes room for the new.

It opens the possibility of once again praising God, not falsely or mechanically, but from the heart. Only when longing for redemption from the ravages of sickness and war is intense can the seeds of renewed hope for the coming of God's justice and peace take root. Rachel's lament is not contrary to praise but the precondition of authentic praise. This is a journey I am on. I am moving from sickness to new life. It is a journey the friars of the province are on. It is a journey many are on. Before we can sing Mary's song we have to face the shadow side and cry out to God for healing.

The picture of Mary we have is drawn in large measure from the Gospel of Luke. In chapter 1 we read:

> In the sixth month the angel Gabriel was sent by God to a town in Galilee called Nazareth, to a virgin betrothed to a man named Joseph, of the House of David; and the virgin's name was Mary. He went in and said to her, "Rejoice, so highly favoured! The Lord is with you."

7

She was deeply disturbed by these words and asked herself what this greeting could mean, but the angel said to her, "Mary, do not be afraid; you have won God's favour. Listen! You are to conceive and bear a son, and you must name him Jesus. He will be great and will be called Son of the Most High. The Lord God will give him the throne of his ancestor David: he will rule over the House of Jacob for ever and his reign will have no end."

Mary said to the angel, "But how can this come about, since I am a virgin?"

"The Holy Spirit will come upon you" the angel answered "and the power of the Most High will cover you with its shadow. And so the child will be holy and will be called Son of God. Know this too: your kinswoman Elizabeth has, in her old age, herself conceived a son, and she whom people called barren is now in her sixth month, *for nothing is impossible to God.*"

"I am the handmaid of the Lord," said Mary "let what you have said be done to me." And the angel left her.

(Lk 1:26-38)

As a young woman Mary probably dreamt dreams about her future and what form it would take. Now her dreams are interrupted. The great silence of God over the centuries has now been ruptured. Initially she was afraid but was receptive of the angel's message. When we read she was deeply disturbed the Greek word used by St. Luke indicates a profound '... shuddering inside and intense anxiety. She is re-assured when she is told that "the Lord" is with her and she consents to what God asks of her. Her source of joy and strength is with God.

The next scenes show Mary going to visit her cousin Elizabeth who is also found to be with child. We read:

'... Mary set out at that time and went as quickly as she could to a town in the hill country of Judah. She went into Zechariah's house and greeted Elizabeth. Now as soon as Elizabeth heard Mary's greeting, the child leapt in her womb and Elizabeth was filled with the Holy Spirit.

She gave a loud cry and said, "Of all women you are the most blessed, and blessed is the fruit of your womb. Why should I be honoured with a visit from the mother of my Lord? For the moment your greeting reached my ears, the child in my womb leapt for joy.

Yes, blessed is she who believed that the promise made her by the Lord would be fulfilled."

(Lk 1: 39-45)

In Mary's visit to Elizabeth we see the pregnant women as the special bearers of God's word. Tina Beattie gives an insight into the love and joy that is in this meeting (*Rediscovering Mary*, p. 42f).

I imagine she does this with a certain mischievous glint in her eye, pointing out what male commentators missed down through the centuries. She says the visitation has often been portrayed in a way that reinforces a certain dreary image of women as submissive and dutiful caregivers, with the young Mary ignoring her own discomfort to go and help her older cousin. Tina imagines Mary setting out with wings on her feet to seek the companionship of the one person in all the world who would understand the uniqueness of her situation and who would share in the delight of her pregnancy. In Mary and Elizabeth we see the power of a love and friendship that was not a duty or a burden but a joyful expression of mutually affirming love.

This is in stark contrast to the disciples of Jesus who were often locked in competition with one another for the first place. The "will to power" is often more in evidence than the *"will to love"*.

Mary then sings her song of praise:

"My soul proclaims the greatness of the Lord
and my spirit exults in God my saviour;
because he has looked upon his lowly handmaid.
Yes, from this day forward all generations will call be blessed,
For the Almighty has done great things for me.
Holy is his name,
And his mercy reaches from age to age for those who fear him.
He has shown the power of his arm,
He has routed the proud of heart.
He has pulled down princes from their thrones and exalted the
lowly.
The hungry he has filled with good things, the rich sent empty away.
He has come to the help of Israel his servant, mindful of his mercy
-according to the promise he made to our ancestors –
of his mercy to Abraham and to his descendants for ever."

Mary stayed with Elizabeth for three months and then went back home.

(Lk 1: 46-56)

This great song of praise is also contrary to many conventional portrayals. It is far from a naïve acceptance

10

of things as they are. Mary rejoices that God has overturned the injustice of the world, has lifted up the poor and satisfied the hungry. Rachel's lament is an act of faithfulness making room for authentic praise. Mary's praise is steeped in prophetic faith. Rachel's lament and her refusal of consolation await the time of new praise of God. Mary's praise and exultation are fully aware of the reality of pain and loss. Mary, like Rachel will lose her child and the sword of grief will pierce her own heart. The evangelist Matthew weaves together the griefs of Rachel and Mary. When their son is still an infant, Mary and Joseph flee with him to Egypt to escape the genocidal law of Herod. As the evangelist tells the story of this flight, he reminds us of Rachel's cry: we hear her voice once again weeping bitterly and refusing all consolation. This is Matthew's account of the flight into Egypt:

'… After they had left, the angel of the Lord appeared to Joseph in a dream and said, "Get up, take the child and his mother with you, and escape into Egypt, and stay there until I tell you, because Herod intends to search for the child and do away with him." So Joseph got up and, taking the child and his mother with him, left that night for Egypt, where he stayed until Herod was dead. This was to fulfil what the Lord had spoken through the prophet:

I called my son out of Egypt

Herod was furious when he realised that he had been outwitted by the wise men, and in Bethlehem and its surrounding district he had all the male children killed who were two years old or under, reckoning by the date he had been careful to ask the wise men. It was then that the words spoken through the prophet Jeremiah were fulfilled:

11

> A voice was heard in Ramah,
> Sobbing and loudly lamenting;
> It was Rachel weeping for her children,
> Refusing to be comforted
> Because they were no more.
>
> *(Matthew 2:13-18)*

Rachel and Mary are bound together as sisters in faith in the biblical tradition. Even though Rachel has often been forgotten and Mary remembered the two belong together in prayer and the practice of Christian faith. Together they remind us that praise without lament can be false. As Emily Dickinson pointed out: "Pain – is missed – in Praise". We have to grow through pain to find healing. Mary and Rachel also remind us that lament without praise is hopelessness. Lament is not meant to affirm us as victims. It is rather a cry for new life, healing and the reign of justice. Mary and Rachel are our two sisters whose prayers accompany us on our healing journey.

The Brothers:

Von Balthasar in reading his favourite christian authors would say that their insight was far ahead of what he and his fellow theologians were trying to say of God. Freud, too would say that what he was exploring in medicine and mental illness had already been explored in the great works of literature down through the ages. One author who did all this for me is the Russian author, Fydor Dostoyevsky. He did this in many ways in his masterpiece entitled: 'The Brothers Karamazov'. There is one incident in the book I refer to here. It comes in Book 2, chapter 5 where the holy man, the *staretz*, Zossima, greets a devout woman who came to him. At first glance this chapter appears as a digression, but the author develops many themes here that will reappear throughout the course of the novel. The digression provides insight into what is going on in the whole novel.

As Dostoyevsky was beginning work on the novel, his own son, Alyosha, died as an infant. Dostoyevsky closed a letter to his brother, Nikolai, with the words "Goodbye, Kilya, pity Alyosha. ... I never felt so sad." Shortly afterwards Anna Grigorevna, his wife, sent her grieving husband in the company of the philosopher Vladamir Solovyov, to the monastery of Optina Pustyn.

The words of comfort uttered by the famous elder, the *staretz,* Father Amvrosy, are echoed in the monk Zossima. In the story of the woman who lost her son Dostoyevsky pours out his own story. The real-life words, spoken in private to Dostoyevsky, are scattered in the fictional, created world of the 'Brothers' before they enter our real world by being read.

The bereft mother who comes to Zossima uses a language full of words and phrases which are repeated over and over again. This doesn't grate on the reader as the reader finds himself or herself empathising with the woman. She uses phrases like the following: "my little boy"; "I can't forget him". She encapsulates his preciousness through the following expressions that evoke his presence which has now become an absence: "his little clothes, his little shirt, his little boots ... all his little things." It's a place of grief and loss that we can relate to in different ways.

In her great grief, she asks not for her beloved child to return, but only to see him from a distance, one more time. Here Dostoyevsky indirectly conveys the infinitude of parental love which is always a reflection and a sharing in divine love:

13

'And if only I could look upon him one little time, if only I could peep at him one little time, without going up to him, without speaking, if I could be hidden in a corner and only see him one little minute, hear him playing in the yard, calling in his little voice, "Mummy, where are you?" If only I could hear him pattering with his little feet about the room just once, only once; for so often, so often I remember how he used to run to me and shout and laugh, if only I could hear his little feet I should know him! But he's gone, Father, he's gone, and I shall never hear him again.'

(p. 52)

As she laments his death, she brings him poignantly to life for us. The image of the mother, whose entire being longs to hold her child again tight in an embrace, and yet only asks to see him from a distance, strikes a nerve in the sensitive reader and conveys the essence of the novel.

Zossima first consoles her with conventional church wisdom. It's something many of us know too well. When confronted by deep tragedy we fall back on conventional wisdom but see in the hurt of the eyes looking at us that our words miss the mark. Zossima says:

'Now listen to me, Mother,' said the elder. 'Once, a long time ago, a great saint saw a woman like you in a church. She was weeping for her little infant child, her only one, whom God had also taken. "Don't you know," said the saint to her, "how bold and fearless these little ones are before the throne of the Lord? There's none bolder or more fearless than they in the Kingdom of Heaven: Thou, O Lord, hast given us life, they say to God, and no sooner had we looked upon it than thou didst take it away. And so boldly and fearlessly do they

14

ask and demand an explanation that God gives them at once the rank of angels. And therefore," said the saint, "you, too, Mother, rejoice and do not weep, for your little one is now with the Lord in the company of his angels."

That's what the saint said to the weeping mother in the olden days. And he was a great saint and he would not have told her an untruth.
Know, then, you too, Mother, that your little one is most assuredly standing now before the throne of the Lord, and is rejoicing and happy, and praying to God for you. And, therefore, weep not, but rejoice."
The woman listened to him with a bowed head, her cheek resting on her hand. She heaved a deep sigh.

(Brothers, p. 53)

The woman is a believer. She has not lost her faith yet Zossima's answer offers her no comfort. Divine justice pales before the enormity of earthly injustice and loss. Thus the grieving woman prefigures the complex rebellion of Ivan Karamazov against God and the world he created where the innocent, particularly children, suffer.

Zossima quickly abandons standard 'conventional' church wisdom and reaches into the biblical past and into the depths of his own heart to offer her counsel. "It is Rachel of old... weeping for her children and will not be comforted because they are not." Such is the last act on earth for you mothers. Be not comforted. Consolation is not what you need. Weep, and be not consoled, but weep.' (Brothers, p.54)

Rachel's lost children remind us of the innocent ones smitten such as Job's children and Jesus on the cross. Zossima tells the woman that when she weeps '... in the end your weeping will turn into quiet joy and your bitter tears will be only the tears of quiet, tender joy, purifying the heart.' Here Dostoyevsky echoes the epigraph of the novel. The epigraph reads:

> Verily, verily, I say unto you,
> Except a corn of wheat fall into the ground
> And die, it abideth alone: but if it die,
> It bringeth forth much fruit.

> *(St John XII, 24)*

Her cross is her grief and it is in taking up her cross that she will eventually come to new life. Rachel's lament will become Mary's song. In the world of psychology Elizabeth Kubler-Ross noticed the different stages those who are dying go through before they become reconciled to their fate. It is in facing and bearing our cross that we open the way for God's transformation and healing.

St Francis and Rachel:

The picture of St. Francis presented to me has often been over-romanticised. I do not believe it is possible to know another person totally let alone one touched by grace as was St. Francis. There is always something infinitely mysterious about the other which I can never understand. One look can never see the whole picture but each angle I look at reveals a new beauty which enriches me. I can never know the real Francis totally but I can let his life speak to me.

St Francis certainly loved Mary, the Mother of Jesus. In the office of the Passion, which he composed, each hour of the office opens by honouring Mary. If Francis prayed the Office every day, then he would have recited the salutation fourteen times daily:

16

Holy Virgin Mary,
There is no one like you
Among the women born in the world.
Daughter and servant
Of the most high and supreme King
And of the Father in Heaven,
Mother of our most holy Lord Jesus Christ,
Spouse of the Holy Spirit,
Pray for us
With Saint Michael the Archangel,
All the powers of heaven
And all the saints,
To your most holy beloved Son,
Our Lord and Master.

Francis begins his greetings in words reminiscent of those of Elizabeth, "Blessed are you among women" (Luke 1:42), or of Jesus himself, "There is no one greater born of women" (Luke 7:25). The text also shows the influence of a simple prayer used in Francis' times: "O Virgin Mary, among the women of the world, there is none like you, a flower like a rose, a fragrance like a lily, pray for us to your Son."

The question remains: *Did Francis know Rachel's song?* There are many incidents recounted in the lives of Francis by Celeno that show he knew the place of loneliness, confusion and not getting things right. In the second life by Celano there is the following story:

(CHAPTER XXVII)

Of the house at the Portiuncula which he started to destroy.

Once when a chapter had to be held at St Mary of the Portiuncula and the time was already at hand, the people of Assisi, seeing that there was no house there, very quickly built a house for the chapter, without the knowledge and in the absence of the man of God. Upon his return, the father looked at the house and took it ill and bewailed it in no gentle tones. Then he himself went up first to destroy the house: he got up on the roof and with strong hands tore off the slates and tiles. He also commanded the brother to come up and to tear down completely this monstrous thing contrary to poverty. For he used to say that whatever might have the appearance of arrogance in that place would quickly spread throughout the order and be accepted as a model by all. He therefore would have destroyed the house to its very foundations, except that a knight who was standing by cooled the ardor of his spirit when he said that the house belonged to the commune and not to the brothers.

This shows an angry Francis not getting things right. Elsewhere in Celano's lives are stories of Francis wrestling with anxiety, low self-esteem and depression. Franciscan joy was born from these experiences.

This transformation of negative experiences into sources of joy is best illustrated by the story of the 'Canticle of the Creatures'. Towards the end of his life Francis returned to Assisi and went to a roughly-made cell outside San Damiano. His companions tell us that his eyesight had deteriorated so that he could not bear the light of the sun during the day or the light of fire at night. What little sleep he was able to enjoy was interrupted by the field mice that ran over him in his cell. The companions tell us of one night in particular when Francis endured a terrible temptation against faith. Feeling sorry for himself he said: "Lord, help me in my infirmities so that I may have the strength to bear them patiently." He then heard: "Tell me brother if in compensation for your suffering and tribulation you were given an immense and precious treasure: the whole mass of the earth changed into pure gold, pebbles into precious stones, and the waters of the rivers into perfume, would you not regard the pebbles and the water as nothing compared to such a treasure? Would you not rejoice?"

"Lord," he replied, "it would be a very great, very precious and inestimable treasure beyond all that one can love and desire."

"Well, brother," the voice said, "be glad and joyful in the midst of all your infirmities and tribulations. As of now, live in peace as if you were already sharing my kingdom."

When Francis came out of that experience he said to his companions:

If the emperor gave a kingdom to one of his servants, how joyful the servant would be! But if he gave him the whole empire, would he not rejoice all the more? I should, therefore, be full of joy in my infirmities and tribulations, seek my consolation in the Lord, and give thanks to God the Father, to his only Son our Lord Jesus Christ, and to the blessing that he has condescended in his mercy to assure me, his poor and unworthy servant, still living on earth, that I would share his kingdom. Therefore, for his glory, for my consolation, and the edification of my neighbour, I wish to compose a new Praises of the Lord for his creatures. These creatures minister to our needs every day; without them we could not live; and through them the human race greatly offends the Creator. Every day we fail to appreciate so great a blessing by not

19

praising as we should the Creator and dispenser of all these gifts.

At this point he broke out in singing the *'Canticle of the Creatures'*:

Most High, all-powerful, good Lord,
Yours are the praises, the glory, the honour and all blessing,
To You alone, Most High, do they belong,
And no one is worthy to mention Your name.

Praise be You, my Lord, with all Your creatures,
Especially Sir Brother Sun,
Who is the day and through whom You give us light,
And he is beautiful and radiant with great splendour;
And bears a likeness of You, Most High One.

Praised be You, my Lord, through Sister Moon
and the stars,
In heaven You formed them clear and precious
and beautiful.

Praised be You, my Lord, through Brother Wind,
And through the air, cloudy and serene, and every kind of
Weather,
Through whom You give sustenance to Your creatures.

Praised be You, my Lord, through Sister Water,
Who is very useful and humble and precious and chaste.

Praise be You, my Lord, through Brother Fire,
Through whom You light the night
And he is beautiful and playful and robust and strong.

Praised be You, my Lord, through our Sister Mother
Earth,
Who sustains and governs us,
And who produces various fruits with coloured flowers
and Herbs.

Praise and bless my Lord and give Him thanks
And serve Him with great humility.
(cf. the Legend of Perugia, p.1258)

He turned his distress and depression into the hands of
God and his sorrow was transformed into a canticle of
praises. Once again Rachel's cry becomes Mary's song.

CHAPTER 2: Facing the Darkness

Walter Brueggamann is one of the leading lights in the study of the Old Testament. His work is a rich source of inspiration for scholars, and people of prayer. In 1985, he wrote two important essays in the *Catholic Theological Quarterly.* One was on the subject of the shape of Old Testament theology in the sense of structure legitimisation. This is the majority voice that we hear, but in his next essay he points out there is another direction in Old Testament that is in conflict with the majority voices. He calls this essay the *'Embrace of Pain'.* There is a failure and restlessness in the life of Israel and its people. This pain is poured out in Israel's practice of lament. Israel's way of lament protests against pain. Israel's voice in the face of pain and injustice will not be embraced. It is a risk that Israel takes hoping for a new road of faith between Yahweh and Israel. The laments are refusals to settle for the way things are. They are acts of relentless hope that believe no situation falls outside Yahweh's capacity for transformation. No situation falls outside the sphere of Yahweh, God.

Moses is one of the first to model this protest. Moses is a bold man who presses God to embrace and deal with the pain. He calls on God to be with us in the fray. The prayers of Moses are radical and dangerous protests that throw down the gauntlet to God:

'...Alas, this people have sinned a great sin; they have made for themselves gods of gold. But now, if thou wilt forgive their sin – and if not, blot me, I pray thee, out of thy book that thou has written.

(Ex. 32:31-32)

22

If thy presence will not go with me, do not carry us up from here.

(Exod. 33:15)

Moses was displeased. Moses said to the Lord, "Why has thou dealt ill with thy servant? And why have I not found favor in thy sight, that thou dost lay the burden of all these people upon me? Did I conceive all this people? Did I bring them forth, that thou shouldst say to me, 'Carry them in your bosom, as a nurse carries the sucking child, to the land which thou didst swear to give their fathers? Where am I to get meat to give to all this people? For they weep before me and say, 'Give us meat, that we may eat.' I am not able to carry all this people alone, the burden is too heavy for me. If thou wilt deal thus with me, kill me at once, if I find favor in thy sight, that I may not see my wretchedness."

(Num. 11:10-15)

In the psalter we hear the voice of Psalm 88. It is a dangerous, unresolved and most desolate of all the laments. It was used by William Styron in *Sophie's Choice*, to articulate the depth of despair by his central character, Stingo: 'Dat is one fine Psalm' (p.505). William Styron himself battled against depression (he said the word 'depression' was a wimp of a word!). Through his books he tried to come to terms with his despair and obviously Ps 88 meant much to him. So in the life of Israel they faced pain and despair and called out to God – the face of pain, failure and near-despair.

In later Jewish reflection on the Hebrew bible these minority voices took on more prominence. In the Targamim and later rabbinic reflection on the scripture in the form of what was called *Midrashim,* the minority voices showed what was really going on with the people when they faced painful situations.

Sigmund Freud, along with Marx and Nietzsche, came to be regarded as the masters of suspicion of what they had been handed down. Freud would have regarded himself as being behind organised religion, he did not believe anymore, yet in a paradoxical way he showed himself to be a sharer in his people's heritage. In the area of mental health he emphasised the importance of articulating the pain felt inside. This was loyal to the tradition of lament. The form of the so-called Freudian-slip was often the key to what we needed to deal with in our lives. The embrace of pain in the Hebrew Bible is now something that has been introduced into the area of psychology and psychoanalysis (Freud's so-called *'talking therapy'*).

Embracing the pain can be an ambiguous term. It can smack of masochism. For the Hebrews and in my own life, pain and failure often entered as uninvited guests. They involve situations and hurt emotions that have to be worked through. That is the sense in which I embrace the pain. In my own life I have had to deal with trauma, depression, anxiety and much personal failure. Healing only began when I could speak of these things in an accepting environment. I know many others who have their own stories of hurt emotions and broken dreams. In religious life there are many who have experienced deep loneliness and compensated for this loneliness in alcohol or disastrous sexual liaisons. The problems of gay men in a male, celibate community is hardly even acknowledged let alone addressed. Failure to face up and own hurt emotions, loneliness and broken dreams leads to much tragedy both for the individual concerned and those with whom he comes into contact. *"Denial is not a river in Egypt"*. It is only by articulating pain in an environment of acceptance that we can deal with the shadow-side of ourselves both as individuals and as a Province.

George Bernanos diagnoses the human condition. He once said that he was not a holy man himself but had a gift of writing about holiness and its heroic expression in daily life. In his work entitled *'The Diary of a Country Priest'*, he spoke of the block that is found in every soul.

He said that in each of us is a secret hatred of ourselves and disturbingly he tells us that it is easier than one thinks to hate oneself. It is easy for many of us to feel self-loathing or to be angry at a world we cannot relate to. In his work entitled: 'La Liberte, pourquoi faire?', he says:

> There is in man a secret, incomprehensible hatred, not only of his fellowmen, but of himself. We can give this mysterious feeling whatever origin or explanation we want, but we must give it one. As far as we Christians are concerned, we believe that this hatred reflects another hatred, a thousand times more profound and lucid: the hatred of the ineffable spirit who was the most resplendent of all the luminaries of the abyss and who will never forgive us his cataclysmic fall. Outside the hypothesis of original sin, this is, of an intrinsic contradiction within our nature, the notion of man does become quite clear, only it is no longer the notion *of man*. When this occurs, man has gone straight through the definitions of man, like a handful of sand running between his fingers.

> *(Liberté, pp 252-253)*

And in another place he writes:

> At its climax, every form of madness succeeds in baring the bottommost foundation of man's soul – that secret

self-hatred that is the deepest part of his life, and probably of every life.

(Un Mauvais Rêve, p. 232-238)

Paul Tillich speaks of faith as being the courage to accept acceptance *(The Courage to Be)*. Many of us do not accept ourselves as we are and this obstructs our view of God who loves us even in our broken condition.

It is only by facing the loneliness and pain of our condition that we open the door of hope, to accept acceptance.

"...In order to meet hope we must first go to the other side of despair. When you trudge on to the very end of the night, you meet another dawn... Optimism is a false hope, made to console cowards and imbeciles. Hope is a virtue and, virtues, a heroic resolution of the soul. The highest form of hope is despair that has been overcome..."

(Liberté, p. 14)

Here Bernanos echoes St Paul's hoping against all hope: Rom 4:18. In my experience of depression and paranoia I know the meaning of his words on the 'self-hatred' that is part of us. I was also interested to note that St. Francis, too, had moments when he had to battle with a negative self-image, that deep hatred of self. In 2 Celano, 115 there is the following story:

Of the saint's temptations and how he overcame temptation

115 As the merits of St Francis increased, so too did his struggle with the ancient serpent. For the greater the gifts bestowed upon him, the more subtle were the temptations and the more serious the assaults hurled against him. Though the devil had often proved him to

26

be a man of war and a strenuous battler and one who did not let up in the struggle for even an hour, nevertheless he always tried to attack his always-victorious foe. At one time there was a temtation of the spirit, of course for the increase of his crown. He was in anguish as a result; and filled with sorrows, he tormented and tortured his body, he prayed and he wept bitterly.

After being thus assailed for several years, he was praying one day at St. Mary of the Portiuncula when he heard a voice within his spirit saying: "Francis, if you have faith like a mustard seed, you will say to this mountain, 'Remove from here and it will remove.' The saint replied: 'Lord, what mountain do you want me to remove?" And again he heard: "The mountain is your temptation." And weeping, Francis said: "Let it be unto me, Lord, as you have said." Immediately all the temptation was driven out and he was made free and put completely at peace within himself.

St Seraphim of Sarov, called the Russian St. Francis, would say that when one soul found peace a thousand would be saved. As Francis was healed of his temptation to believe he was not loved, so he was able to radiate the love of God to others.

That is the journey we are on in this world. I am myself, and those who join me as broken sinners round the cross. The meditations on lament are a form of shared prayer where we express our brokenness, our failures in faith before the cross.

THE BOOK OF LAMENTATIONS

In John Updike's novel (*Rabbit Run*, p237) he describes his famous everyman, Rabbit Angstron, thus:

> Harry has no taste for the dark tangled, visceral aspect of Christianity, the going through quality of it, the passage into death and suffering that redeems and inverts these things, like an umbrella blowing inside out. He lacks the mindful will to walk the straight line of a paradox. His eyes turn toward the light however it glances into the retina.

Harry stands for many people I know and many times I feel myself as one of these people. I would like to avoid suffering, turning towards any light or escape that comes across my path. Yet the gospel boldly sets the cross of Christ as the centre of its message and it also accepts the cross of discipleship. Difficulties and sufferings are not problems for which the gospel provides an escape but part of a reality that the Christian experiences and in which Christians share a faith by encouraging one another in hope. In the story of Jacob wrestling with the angel at Peniel, he holds despair before God and confidence in a tight embrace. With the morning there comes a blessing (Gen 32: 23-32).

The Book of Lamentations:

The Book of Lamentations gives a voice to despair before God while all the time awaiting his response. 2 Kings 25 is the historical setting for the book. All the events mentioned in 2 Kings25 are found in the poems of Lamentations. In

587 B.C. the holy city Jerusalem fell to Babylonian armies. The leaders and many of the people were marched six hundred miles away into exile. It was a disaster and suffering on a monumental scale occurred. Lamentations is a funeral service for the city. After the fall, carnage was rampant, cannibalism and sacrilege were found everywhere and the innocent children were murdered ('Rachel'). The worst that can happen to body and spirit happened here – a nadir of suffering:

Look, O Lord, and see!
With who have thou dealt thus?
Should women eat their offspring,
The children of their tender care?
Should priest and prophet be slain
In the sanctuary of the Lord?

In the dust of the streets
Lie the young and the old;
My maidens and my young men
Have fallen by the sword;
In the day of thy anger thou hast slain them,
Slaughtering without mercy.

Thou didst invite as to the day of
An appointed feast
My terrors on every side;
And on the day of the anger of the Lord
None escaped or survived;
Those whom I dandled and reared
My enemy destroyed.

(2:20-22)

Israel kept the experience of the fall of Jerusalem current by remembering the event in an annual act of worship – a feast on the ninth of Ab. The book pays attention to the exact ways in which suffering takes place and turns these sufferings into laments before God calling for his help. The form of the laments is what is called an acrostic form. Each line begins with a letter of the Hebrew alphabet – we would say in English, all the emotions A-Z, in Hebrew it would read all the emotions from Aleph to Tau. The author or authors of Lamentations are unknown, even though a later tradition ascribed it to Jeremiah. This has now been abandoned.

The first poem begins by describing what Zion's troubles look like from the outside:

> How lonely sits the city
> That was full of people

(1:1)

It ends by crying out what it feels like from the inside:

> Is it nothing to you, all you who pass by?
> Look and see
> If there is any sorrow like my sorrow
> Which was brought upon me."

(1:12)

The second chapter extends the rage of suffering into the area of divine wrath. No emotion is more unpleasant or more difficult to face than anger. It is something we prefer to repress or deny exists at all. The denial of anger takes revenge on our moral and physical health. Chapter 2 explores the area of divine anger. God is not seen as a remote deity but as someone who is distressed and angry with his people when they turn from him to destructive behaviour. He cares enough to be angry with his people, to take them seriously. The desire to whitewash, to avoid, to euphemise God's anger is completely rejected. God's anger and its consequences are faced squarely:

> How the Lord in his anger
> Has set the daughter of Zion under a cloud!
>
> The Lord has become like an enemy,
> He has destroyed Israel;
> He has destroyed all its palaces,
> Laid in ruins its strongholds;
> And he has multiplied in the daughter of Judah
> Mourning and lamentation.

> **(2:5)**

In the third poem a man appears who laments as an individual. The result is an expression of despair at its deepest, at the personal level:

> I am the man who has seen affliction
> Under the rod of his wrath.

> *(3:1)*

No longer is the lament being conducted from the outside looking in.

> Beth: "He has wasted my flesh and skin away,
> He has broken my bones,
> He has made a yoke for me,
> He has encircled by head with weariness.
> He has forced me to dwell in darkness,
> With the dead of long ago."

> *(2:4-6)*

Chapter 4 again looks at the pain but from a distance:

> "How the gold has grown dim,
> How the pure gold is changed!
> The holy stones he scattered
> At the head of every street.

(4:1)

The fifth chapter is a prayer to Yahweh, God, and places the entire lament before God. It begins:

> Yahweh, remember what has happened to us:
> Look on us and see our degradation.
> Our inheritance has passed to aliens,
> Our homes to barbarians.
> We are orphans, we are fatherless:
> Our mothers are like widows.

(5:1-3)

All through the laments there lies a wrestling with near-despair while all the time keeping faith that God hears.

In the personal lament of Chapter 3 there is the cry of faith in the midst of despair:

> *Zain:* Brooding on my anguish and affliction
> Is gall and wormwood.
> My spirit ponders it continually
> And sinks within me.
> This is what I shall tell my heart,
> And so recover hope:
>
> *Heth:* The favours of Yahweh are not all past,
> His kindness is not exhausted;
> Every morning they are renewed;

Great is his faithfulness.
'My portion is Yahweh,' says my soul
'And so I will hope in him.'

(3:19-24)

However, chapter 5 ends with the words:

'Make us come back to you, Yahweh,
And we will come back.
Renew our days as in times past,
Unless you have utterly rejected us,
In an anger that knows no limits.'

(5:21-22)

Despair and hope are still wrestling and here the poems end. There is no voice heard from Yahweh God, no answer. It is the season for lament in profound loneliness.

Elie Wiesel, the winner of the 1986 Nobel Peace Prize, is a living embodiment of the journey of lamentations. He is also a modern Job-like figure who rebels against and questions God.

As a child he was taken prisoner to the death camps in Auschwitz and Buchenwald. He describes here how his faith in God disappeared in his disturbing account of his time in the camps in his book 'Night':

Never shall I forget that night, the first night in camp, which has turned my life into one long night, seven times cursed and seven times sealed. Never shall I forget that smoke. Never shall I forget the little faces of the children, whose bodies I saw turned into wreaths of smoke beneath a silent blue sky.
Never shall I forget those flames, which consumed my faith forever.

Never shall I forget that nocturnal silence which deprived me, for all eternity, of the desire to live. Never shall I forget those moments, which murdered my God and my soul and turned my dreams to dust. Never shall I forget these things, even if I am condemned to live as long as God Himself does. Never. (p. 45)

Later on he describes how God died for him when he was forced to watch the death of a 12-year-old boy. In the section quoted above the flames that consumed the innocent consumed his faith.

After the war he met the French Catholic writer, Francois Mauriac. Mauriac confessed how he saw the innocent children being led away and how he was full of grief. Elie told him that he was one of those children. All both men could do was weep and pour out their lament in the season of loneliness. God seemed truly absent.

However, Wiesal never ceased to wrestle with the despair he experienced in the camps. He tried to explore in his literature alternate ways of looking at his experience. In his work the *'Gates of the Forest'*, he includes the following beautiful lines:

"It's inhuman to wall yourself up in pain and memories as if in prison. Suffering must open us to others. It must not cause us to reject them. The Talmud tells us that God suffers with man. Why? In order to strengthen the bonds between creation and Creator; God chooses to suffer in order to better understand man and be better understood by him. But you, you insist upon suffering alone. Such suffering shrinks you, diminishes you. Friend, that is almost cruel." (p. 180)

In his lament he is beginning to wrestle with hope in the one he thought he lost forever. Despair had not ceased to wrestle with hope.

In much of his career Wiesel has tried to bring God to count for all travesties that exist against humanity. In an article written for the New York Times, October, 2nd, 1997 he shows signs of coming to peace again with God. He asks whether the enemies of Auschwitz wanted to destroy God along with the Jews. Now he wonders: "Ought we not think of your pain too? Watching your children suffer at the hands of your children. Haven't you also suffered?"

He confesses to longing to "make up" and experience God's loving presence and companionship again. He still questioned God as to where he was when his "... children were marked for limitation, isolation and death." Yet now he is coming to see that God suffered with those who suffered. After his period of lament and Job-like rebellion Wiesel is coming to know God all over again. This is the journey the Book of Lamentations launches us on.

The Book of Lamentations helped the people as individuals embrace their pain. Embraced pain enabled new beginnings. Yahweh did answer, if not immediately. In the heart of their despair in exile the voice of Deutero – Isaiah could be heard. The prayers of Zion in lamentations are shown to have reached Yahweh. Through the voice of the prophet, Yahweh says:

"For Zion was saying, 'Yahweh has abandoned me,
The Lord has forgotten me,'
Does a woman forget her baby at the breast,
Or fail to cherish the son of her womb?
I will never forget you.
See I have branded you on the palms of my hands,
Your ramparts are always under my eye."

(Is 49:14-16)

Psalm 88 – Darkness:

The Book of Lamentations was very like Jacob wrestling with God – despair confronting hope. Ps. 88 is much darker than this. It is the psalm of unrelieved suffering. It looks despair in the face. In Jerusalem at St. Peter in Gallicantu, it is the psalm especially chosen for that place.   St. Peter's look of betrayal was the last look Jesus would have seen.

My own favourite version of Ps. 88 is one we use in the breviary. The super-scription used when we pray the psalm is 'This is your hour, this is the reign of darkness,'

(Lk 22:53)

The psalm begins:

Lord my God, I call for help by day;
I cry at night before you.

Let my prayer come into your presence,
O turn your ear to my cry.
For my soul is filled with evils;
My life is on the brink of the grave.
I am reckoned as one in the tomb;
I have reached the end of my strength.

Like one alone among the dead;
Like the slain lying in their graves;
Like those you remember no more,
Cut off, as they are, from your hand.

You have laid me in the depths of the tomb;
In places that are dark, in the depths,.
Your anger weighs down upon me:
I am drowned beneath your waves.

The words, *'I cry out'* or *'call on help'* are a translation of a Hebrew verb that indicates anguish and distress (Ps 107: 6, 28). The cry of Ps. 88 provides no answers, only deeper loneliness and profound questioning. It reflects the cries of Job (Job 19: 9-15) as he faces his isolation and loss.

Unrelieved suffering is the hurt of some people. They seem to share in some mysterious way in the 'suffering-servant'. Robert Davidson, who wrote on the psalms, visited a friend of his whose child was murdered in Dunblaine. He asked her how she was coping.

She answered: 'I am not coping. I never will.' Her pain was shared by Ann Weems. Her son who had a bright future was murdered on the night of his 21st birthday. This plunged her into a deep depression – both women share Rachel's lament. Ann went to Walter Bruggemann and he introduced her to the prayer of lament. She poured out her feelings in a modern lament. Others who suffer from the same loneliness find solace in her words. In one of her laments she says:

'O God, find me!
I am lost
In the valley of grief,
And I cannot see my way out.

My friends leave baskets of balm
At my feet,
But I cannot bend to touch
The healing
To my heart.
They call me to leave
This valley,
But I cannot follow

The faint sound
Of their voices.
They sing their songs
Of love,
But the words fade
And vanish in the wind.
They knock,
But I cannot find the door.
They shout to me,
But I cannot find the voice
To answer.

O God, find me?
Come into this valley
And find me!
Bring me out of this land
Of weeping.

(Ann Weems, Psalms of Lament, p. 9)

William Styron as we saw used Ps88 to help express Stingo's deep sadness. The character Styron created mirrored his own battle with depression (that 'wimp' of a word) and his battle with suicidal thoughts.

I remember myself after praying this psalm as I lay in hospital as I battled with the night of illness and the seeming loss of God.

Another man who expressed Ps 88 in a modern way, for me, is the poet Philip Larkin. He was a professed atheist who was afflicted with a deep and dark depression. Even though he was an atheist he still snuck into churches at quiet hours and prayed there. In his poem 'Church Going' he describes his clandestine visits thus:

A serious house on serious earth it is,
In whose blent air all our compulsions meet,
Are recognised, and robed as destinies.
And that much never can be obsolete.
Since someone will forever be surprising
A hunger in himself to be more serious,
And gravitating with it to this ground,
Which, he once heard, was proper to grow wise in,
If only that so many dead lie round.

(Church Going)

He expresses the mood of the beginning of Ps, 88 when he tries to reach out to God who remains silent. His haunting poem to the dawn, *Aubade*, expresses the end of Ps. 88 in a modern way. He expresses the loneliness and darkness of those who live in mental turmoil and anguish. He shows the loneliness of his life and the fear of death.

There is at the end of this poem a battle between despair and life:

I work all day, and get half-drunk at night,
Waking at four to soundless dark, I stare.

In time the curtain-edges will grow light.
Till then I see what's really always there:
Unresting death, a whole day nearer now,
Making all thought impossible but how
And where and when I shall myself die.
Arid interrogation: yet the dread
Of dying, and being dead,
Flashes afresh to hold and horrify.

This is a special way of being afraid
No trick dispels. Religion used to try,

That vast moth-eaten musical brocade
Created to pretend we never die,
And specious stuff that says no rational being
Can fear a thing it will not feel, not seeing
That this is what we fear – no sight, no sound,
No touch or taste or smell, nothing to think with,
Nothing to love or link with,
The anaesthetic from which none come round.

All three, Styron, Weems and Larkin, wrestled with the great darkness in their lives. Larkin, towards the end of his days, was offered the position of Poet Laureate but he declined the offer. His inspiration and use of words had dried up he was in even further darkness. The ironic fact is that others in darkness draw courage from the works of all three. The same can be true for all who wrestle with darkness especially in the Order and Province. It is a special way of sharing in the Suffering-Servant vocation. Jacob, after he wrestled with God, suffered the wound in his hip. He became the first wounded healer.

In its ending Ps. 88 stands out from other psalms of lament. They finish on a high note of hope. They express deep anguish, yet end in a cry of life. Ps. 88 is an outsider to lament. It stands alone. Robert Davidson, in his work entitled: *'The Vitality of Worship'* (p. 292) says the Hebrew allows a possible ending of the psalm with the one word – 'Darkness'. It is a time when one lives in profound loneliness with no end in sight.

Yet it is faith in its profound depths to pray in that darkness. Ps. 88 concludes in the following way in the breviary version:

As for me, Lord, I call to you for help:
In the morning my prayer comes before you.

40

Lord why do you reject me?
Why do you hide your face?

Wretched, close to death from my youth,
I have borne your trials, I am numb,
Your fury has swept down upon me;
Your terrors have utterly destroyed me.

They surround me all the day like a flood,
They assail me all together.
Friend and neighbour you have taken away:
My one companion is darkness.

(vv. 13-18)

A Person out of Time:

The Book of Qoheleth (Ecclesiastes) looks at the pain of loss from a different perspective. In Chapter 1 I quoted his piece from chapter 3 where he speaks of each event having its time or season but this is precisely the tragedy of Qoheleth. He cannot find his own time or place.

Qoheleth is a post-exilic wisdom teacher who has seen the old-world disintegrate and explores the effect of that on himself and on his people.

He begins his work with the famous *'Vanity of Vanities'*:

The words of the Teacher, the
Son of David, king in Jerusalem.
Vanity of vanities, says the Teacher,
Vanity of vanities! All is vanity.
What do people gain from all the
Toil
At which they toil under the
Sun?

A generation goes, and a
Generation comes,
But the earth remains forever.
The sun rises and the sun goes
Down,
And hurries to the place where
it rises.
The wind blows to the south,
and goes around to the north;
Round and round goes the wind,
and on its circuits the wind
returns.
All streams run to the sea,
but the sea is not full;
To the place where the streams
flow,
there they continue to flow,
all things are wearisome;
more than one can express;
The eye is not satisfied with
seeing,
or the ear filled with hearing.
What has been is what will be,
and what has been done is
what will be done;

There is nothing new under the
sun.
Is there a thing of which it is
said,
"See, this is new"?
It has already been
in the ages before us.

The people of long ago are not
remembered ,
nor will there be any
remembrance
of people yet to come
by those who come after them.

(Ecc 1:1-12)

The word 'hebel' in Hebrew is translated as 'vanity'. It means something like vapour and it captures something of the sense of ephemerality and futility. Different translators have tried to get the sense of Hebel into English: utterly vain, utterly vain (Moffatt), emptiness, emptiness (NEB), 'futility, utter futility' (REB), it is useless, useless (GNB), utterly absured (Fox). All our work, all our toil (a favourite word for Qoleleth) end up in futility. All is chasing of the wind and ultimately there is nothing new under the sun.

At various stages he encourages his readers to eat, drink and be merry:

"… Go eat your bread with enjoyment and drink your wine with a merry heart for God has always approved what you do. Let your garments always be white: let not evil be lacking on your head."

(9:7)

Yet it seems that the effort is still doomed to end in futility. Pleasure is not lasting:

'…I said to myself: "Come now, I will make a test of pleasure; enjoy yourself." But again, this also was vanity. I said of laughter, "It is mad," and of pleasure, "What use is it?" I searched with my mind how to cheer my body with wine – my mind still guiding me with wisdom

43

– and how to lay hold on folly, until I might see what was good for mortals to do under heaven during the few days of their life.

I made great works; I built houses and planted vineyards for myself; I made myself gardens and parks, and planted in them all kinds of fruit trees. I made myself pools from which to water the forest of growing trees. I bought male and female slaves and had slaves who were born in my house; I also had great possessions of herds and flocks, more than any who had been before me in Jerusalem. I also gathered for myself silver and gold and the treasure of kings and of the provinces; I got singers, both men and women, and delights of the flesh and many concubines.'

(2:1-8)

He has tried to find meaning in pleasure, produce, wealth and sex. Unless God has made the gift then our pursuit of their own is absurdity or vanity, ending up in more loneliness. In 5:2 Qoheleth tells us he sees God as a far-away deity "He in Heaven and we on earth." Once more there is disappointment.

Qoheleth and his vices do have echoes in our modern/post-modern world. The translation of Hebel as absurd can lead us to see parallels with Albert Camus. In his play *'Caligula'* Caligula is faced with the absurd meaning of life that he forces on his subjects. "All I wish is to regain some peace of mind in a world that has regained a meaning." (Caligula, p. 22).

In his work *L'Etranger* (translated as 'The Outsider' or 'The Stranger') we see 'absurdity' in the person of Meursault. He is at zero-point in his life and can no longer cope. He lurches from situation to situation, feeling lost and outside. He gives people the answer he expects they want because he cannot meaningfully engage with the questions. It is only at the end when he rebels against the prison chaplain and accepts his fate that he achieves a kind of peace.

In a later work entitled: *'La Chute'* he explores the theme not so much of fallen men as of falling men in the person of Jean – Baptisie Clamence. He once, in Paris, heard a cry of someone for help but passed quickly by. He abandoned the person who cried and the person threw herself into the Seine. This has always haunted him and he sees his life ever since as being in free-fall. This work is relevant here because Camus wrote it at a time of great distress in his private life. His infidelities had caused his wife to suffer a severe breakdown. His pursuit of pleasure had ended in vanity and hurt for others. *'La Chute'* was his vehicle to articulate his pain.

The American rock singer, Bruce Springstein, at one stage wrestled with the experience of 'vanity' and 'futility'. He gave an interview at the height of his success with the album *'Born in the USA'*. He spoke of a time that changed his life and which preceded his success. He spoke of a time in his life when he felt he had to face himself and answer the question: "Can I live with myself after others had let me down?" and he was determined to face the harder question: "Can I live with myself after I have let others down?" He did not know could he live with these questions. Was it all just vanity or chasing of the wind?

He explored the questions through his music, which ultimately formed the album 'Nebraska', a darker, more sombre offering that his fans had come to expect. He explores how this futility can lead to destructive behaviour in songs like 'Johnny 99' and 'Nebraska'. Oliver Stone in his film entitled: *'Natural Born Killers'* horrified the world when he explored the same theme.

One of the most beautifully written songs in the album

is 'My Father's House'. Here Springsteen explores using his father as an image of how we say and do harsh things that bring us upset and we bear the wounds in our being.

He begins by describing the initial relationship of child to parent:

Last night I dreamed that I was a child
Out where the pines grow wild and tall
I was trying to make it home through the
forest before the darkness falls.

I heard the wind rustling through the trees
and ghostly voices rose from the fields
I ran with my heart pounding down that
broken path
with the devil snappin' at my heels.

I broke through the trees and there in the
night
My father's house stood shining hard and
bright the branches and brambles tore
my clothes and scratched my arms
But I ran till I fell shaking in his arms.

He describes the safe world when things are fine, when he was lone in the dark and finds shelter in his father's arms. Then, far away, he thinks of the things that led to the breakdown in the relationship. He says:

I awoke and I imagined the hard things
that pulled us apart
Will never again, sir, tear us from each
other's hearts
I got dressed and to that house I did ride

from out on the road I could see its
windows shining in the light.

He speaks of the things we say and do to sour relationships.
The same is true for many of us. Springstein goes on to
describe his attempted make-up with his father :

I walked up the steps and stood on the
porch a woman I didn't recognise came
and spoke to me through a chained door
I told her my story and who I'd come for
She said: "I'm sorry son but no one by that
name lives here anymore."

My father's house shines hard and bright
it stands like a beacon calling me in the
night
Calling and calling so cold and alone
Shining cross this dark highway where
our sins lie unatoned.

He sees his father 'cold and calling so cold and alone' which
shines across the highway where our sins lie unatoned.
'Atonement' has the meaning of being at one with the other
in peace, but often times this is unrealised. Qoheleth, for
me, expresses all this sadness in his writings and musings.

At the end of the book is a hauntingly beautiful passage.
He describes the world as he knew now passing away:

'…. In the day when the guards of the house tremble,
and the strong men are bent, and the women who grind
cease working because they are few, and those who
look through the windows see dimly; when the doors on
the street are shut, and the sound of the grinding is low,

47

and one rises up at the shout of a bird, and all the
daughters of song are brought low; when one is afraid
of heights, and terrors are in the road; the almond tree
blossoms, the grasshopper drags itself along and desire
fails; because all must go to their eternal home, and the
mourners will go about the streets; before the silver cord
is snapped, and the golden bowl is broken, and the pitcher
is broken at the fountain, and the wheel broken at the
cistern, and the dust returns to the earth as it was, and
the breath returns to God who gave it. Vanity of vanities,
says the Teacher, all is vanity.'

(Ecc 12: 3-8)

The picture of desolation and sin the passage invokes for
body, household and world itself culminating in the loss of
life itself, is reminiscent of the more desolate landscapes of
Salvador Dali.

Qoheleth shows us the emptiness and absurdity that we
experience in life at some time. The verse quoted above is
a fitting lament for us who have the 'old-world' disappear
and struggle to find who we are in the world today. For me,
Qoheleth gives language and a voice to the dark night so
many experiences when one world passes away and they
have not arrived at a new vision of the world and self.

John of the Cross wrote of the dark night of the soul
when all former consolations are lost and one is
disconcerted, at zero-point: "... [the soul] suffers great pain
and grief since there is added to all this [because of the
solitude and abandonment caused in it by the dark night]
the fact that it finds no consolation or support in anything."
(Dark Night of the Soul, XI, 7). Embraced endings and
pain once again enable new beginnings. Qoheleth helps
articulate the pain of meaninglessness and loss and enables
us, once again, to hear the words of Jesus:

"Come to me, all who are weary and are overburdened
and I will give you rest."

(Mtt 11:28)

Oscar Wilde penned the following lines:

"How else but through a broken heart
May Lord Christ enter in."
(Oscar Wilde, Ballad of Reading Gaol)

Francis and the Embrace of Pain:

St Francis knew the meaning of an old-world view collapsing
before a new one could emerge. At certain stages in his
life he knew the pain of self-loathing before he could come
to the vision of God, revealed in Jesus, through the Spirit.
He had, again and again, to die to the old-self before he
was transformed by grace. When he was a young man
Francis went through many experiences and
disappointments, including imprisonment. His spirit was
never satisfied and it was when he was faced with painful
experiences that he began to seek who he was in God.

Celano tells us the following story of Francis:

For, indeed, while this man was still in the glow of
youthful passion, and the age of wantonness was urging
him on immoderately to fulfill the demands of youth;
and while, not knowing how to restrain himself, he was
stirred by the venom of the serpent of old, suddenly the
divine vengeance, or, perhaps better, the divine mercy,
came upon him and sought first to recall his erring senses

by visiting upon him mental distress and bodily suffering, according to the saying of the prophet: *Behold I will hedge up thy way with thorns, and I will stop it up with a wall.*

Thus, worn down by a long illness, as man's stubbornness deserves when it can hardly be corrected except by punishments, he began to think of things other than he was used to thinking upon.

When he had recovered somewhat and had begun to walk about the house with the support of a cane to speed the recovery of his health, he went outside one day and began to look about at the surrounding landscape with great interest. But the beauty of the fields, the pleasantness of the vineyards, and whatever else was beautiful to look upon, could stir in him no delight.

(1 Cel 3)

Francis never saw pain, illness or failure as being total. He may have been tempted to despair but he never did. In his illness he began to change his way of viewing things. The illness signalled the end of one part of his life before another could be embraced.

The transformation begun in illness and darkness of the spirit ended in release. As Francis grew in God's grace he happened to meet a leper. This group had nauseated Francis at one stage. *(See Testament)* but now he stopped and embraced the leper. In embracing the other he came to himself. Again, the seed that died had yielded a rich harvest.

(John 12:24)

CHAPTER 3: Turning Towards God

Rabbi Abraham Heschel has become an important influence in my life. He is my inspiration for this and the following chapter. He calls the moment of prayer – theotropism. This is our movement towards God. This accounts for this chapter. In his meditation on the prophets he shows God's movement and relation to human beings. This forms the basis of the next meditation and, indeed, the rest of the book.

Rabbi Heschel was a Hasidic Jew who emigrated from Poland a week before Hitler invaded. He lost his family in the death camps. When he came to America he could convince nobody of the plight of European Jewry. He felt an onrush of despair. He prayed and lamented in the Jewish tradition. Eventually he decided he could still pray, teach and write and by teaching people of their dignity before God became a voice that would speak for peace, justice and religious tolerance. He gave his life for this cause.

The analysis of the world he found was in the lines of the Hebrew prophets of old and make compelling reading: Having lost his family in the death camps he wrote the following of our age of violence. He saw in his own lifetime the Vietnam war. In our day we have all the violence of the Middle East and the Sudan. The genius of propaganda has kept the faces of the victim out of sight for the most part so our consciences won't be disturbed. Rabbi Heschel does not let his audience off the hook so easily.

He says:

Emblazoned over the gates of the world in which we live is the escutcheon of the demons. The mark of Cain in the face of man has come to overshadow the likeness of God. There has never been so much guilt and distress, agony and terror. At no time has the earth been so soaked with blood.

(Between God and Man, p. 255)

Addressing a conference on ageing he declares:

I see the sick and the despised, the defeated and the bitter, the rejected and the lonely. I see them clustered together and alone, clinging to a hope for somebody's affection that does not come to pass. I hear them pray for the release that comes with death. I see them deprived and forgotten, masters yesterday, outcasts today.

(The Insecurity of Freedom, p. 70)

In the 1960's Rabbi Heschel continued to find social outlets for his prophetic consciousness. He marched with Martin Luther King and penned the following words in the plight of the black people.

My heart is sick when I think of the anguish and the sighs, of the quiet tears shed in the nights in the overcrowded dwellings in the slums of our great cities, of the pangs of despair, of the cry of humiliation, which is running over.

(The Insecurity of Freedom, p. 88)

Rabbi Heschel was a profound philosopher of religion. He was one of the principal Jewish spokesmen in the dialogue with the church that led to the Vatican II document on

Christian-Jewish relations, *Nostra Aetate*. Pope Paul VI was very taken by the holiness of Rabbi Heschel and went so far as to quote him verbatim in one of his talks. However, Rabbi Heschel was prophetically aware of the shortcomings of the major religions. He had seen his own family exterminated by a society that called itself Christian. Some of the guards at the death camp worshipped in the nearby Carmelite church. In a conference on youth he said the following as a prophetic challenge to the major religions.

He says the problem of youth is not youth:

> The problem is the spirit of our age: denial of transcendence, the vapidity of values, emptiness in the heart. ... Eclipse of sensitivity is the mark of our age. Callousness expands at the rate of nuclear energy, while more sensitivity subsides.
>
> *(The Insecurity of Freedom, p. 37)*

When young people see is harshness, indifference and lack of personal faith commitment they look elsewhere. There is no sense of the sacred or of transcendence or of the beauty and dignity of the human being.

In his work entitled: *'God in Search of Man'*, he criticises religion in an even more stark statement:

> It is customary to blame secular science and anti-religious philosophy for the eclipse of religion in modern society. It would be more honest to blame religion for its own defeats. Religion declined not because it was refuted, but because it became irrelevant, dull, oppressive, and insipid. When faith is completely replaced by creed, worship by discipline, love by habit; when the crisis of today is ignored because of the splendour of

the past; when faith becomes an heirloom rather than a living fountain; when religion speaks only in the name of authority rather than with the voice of compassion – its message becomes meaningless.'

(God in Search of Man, p. 3)

Indifference and callousness mark many people's experience of religion. In our church the abuse of the vulnerable and the indifference and deceit with which those who suffered were treated are the gravest testimony for me of this failure.

Rabbi Heschel points us all back to the realm of prayer. In an article written in 1970 entitled: 'On Prayer', he points to a spiritual blackout, a blackout of God that dominates our age.

What we experience is not only the dark night of the soul but also the dark night of the world. God has been driven out of hearts and minds. "... The spiritual blackout is increasing daily .... We no longer know how to resist the vulgar, how to say 'No' in the face of a higher 'Yes' ... We have lost the sense of the holy." Our world is aflame with arrogant atrocities and rabid terrorism. Our scandalous desecration of the world cries out to the heavens.   In the face of evil we either become "... callous participants" or remain "... indifferent onlookers". The relentless pursuit of our selfish interest make us oblivious to what is going on around us and so nothing or nobody matters unless it can be turned to our own advantage in the service of our self-interests.

Heschel writes of humankind torn between the "...good urge" and the "... evil urge", swinging like a pendulum between what is godly and what is beastly, between the pull towards the divine and the pull towards the selfish, between what is more than human and what is less than human. For Heschel, if we are to live knowingly we must be sensitive to the sanctity of life and to all that is sacred. The sacred is what is ultimately precious, this sensitivity implies sensitivity to "… what is dear to God". There are echoes of Francis Canticle here. Central to Heschel's spirituality is our religious commitment; our openness to God is no mere adjunct to human existence but is at the very heart and core of what it is to be human. Human life is holy because human life is lived in partnership with God. Prayer is our way of entering the divine and letting God in. He says:

> *Prayer is our attachment to the utmost. Without God in sight we are like the scattered rungs of a broken ladder. To pray is to become a ladder on which thoughts mount to God* to join the movement toward Him which surges unnoticed throughout the entire universe.
>
> We do not step out of the world when we pray' we merely see the world in a different setting. The self is not the hub, but the spoke of the revolving wheel. In prayer we shift the centre of living from self-consciousness to self-surrender. God is the centre toward which all forces end. He is the source, and we are the flowing of His force, the ebb and flow of His tides.
>
> *(Man's Quest for God, p. 7)*

Carl Jung coming from a difference perspective corroborates Rabbi Heschel's insights. As his insights into mental illness developed he said our healing depended ultimately on how we related to what he called the 'numinous' or what we call 'God'. The beginnings of this insight can be seen in his treatment of alcoholism. An American businessman known to us as Rowland H., went to Jung for treatment. Jung told him that his situation was hopeless "… unless he could become the subject of a spiritual or religious experience in short a genuine conversion." This statement of Jung's became instrumental in the conversion and cure of Bill Wilson, leading to the foundation of Alcoholics Anonymous in 1934. A correspondence built up between Wilson and Jung. In one of the letters of Jung to Wilson he says the following:

Dear Mr W ….

Those days I had to be exceedingly careful of what I said. I had found out that I was misunderstood in every possible way. Thus I was very careful when I talked to Rowland H.

But what I really thought about was the result of many experiences with men of his kind.

His craving for alcohol was the equivalent, on a low level, of the spiritual thirst of our being for wholeness, expressed in medieval language: the union with God.

How could one formulate such an insight in a language that is not misunderstood in our days?

The only right and legitimate way to such an experience is that it happens to you in reality, and it can only happen to you when you walk on a path, which leads you to higher understanding. ….

I am strongly convinced that the evil principle prevailing in this world leads the unrecognised spiritual need into perdition if it is not counteracted either by real religious insight or by the protective wall of human community. An ordinary man, not protected by an action from above and isolated in society, cannot resist the power of evil, which is called, very aptly, the Devil. But the use of such words arouses so many mistakes that one can only keep aloof from them as much as possible. …

I am risking it with you because I conclude from your very decent and honest letter that you have acquired a point of view above the misleading platitudes one usually hears about alcoholism.

You see, "alcohol" in Latin is *spiritus,* and you use the same word for the highest religious experience as well as for the most depraving poison. The helpful formula therefore is: *spiritus contra spiritum.*

Thanking you again for your kind letter, I remain,
Yours sincerely,
C. G. Jung

Our addictions click in when we lose God on our journey. It is because of his insight that we are at heart religious or spiritual that Jung ultimately broke with his long-time friend and mentor, Sigmund Freud. Freud said that as more the fruits of knowledge became accessible to man, the more widespread in the decline of religious belief. (*Future of an Illusion*).

Jung saw the human being as complex and spiritual and he often hoped the major religions of the world would bring their teachings and practices on healing into a dialogue with his insights from psychiatry and medicine. He did not mean his therapy to replace spirituality but to see his insights integrated into a modern spirituality. It is by letting God in, in all our callousness and failures and dark nights that we are ultimately healed and become wonder healers of others – another insight from Jung.

The Cry of the Spirit:

The artist and writer Samuel Beckett once wrote privately in his German diaries of art and writing – "… The art that is a prayer sets up prayer, releases prayer in the onlooker, i.e. *Priest*: Lord have mercy on us. *People*: Christ have mercy on us." The classification of Beckett as an atheist belongs to other people's mania to categorise and box people. Beckett did not accept these categorisations. These words from his German diary are very powerful for me. I have always seen in art, literature or theatre the cry of humanity for mercy, a prayer to God. In Beckett's play, 'Endgame', a despairing play about despair there is a prayer scene. Hanm asks Clov and Nagg to pray to God. Hanm concludes from the lack of response from the Godhead: "The bastard! He doesn't exist." This line caused outrage. Beckett implied to those who said he should remove these lines " So it no more blasphemes than, "My God, my God, why hast thou forsaken me." When Beckett wrote 'Endgame' he was suffering from anguish and grief after the death of his brother.

The playwright who expresses best for me this plea to God for mercy is Tennessee Williams. He had a traumatic childhood and lived all his life close to brokeness. He sought relief in drugs and wrong relationships but all the time his loneliness haunted him. His sister Rose eventually lost her sanity and suffered the horrors of a lobotomy. Williams saw in her what he feared most in himself. Williams felt that the world was dominated by cruelty in which the innocent are either destroyed or corrupted. His plays, 'The Glass Menagerie' and 'A Streetcar named Desire' demonstrate this all too dramatically. Laura ('Rose') in 'The Glass Menagerie', lives in a world of fear and when she reaches out for love is crushed.

In 'A Streetcar named Desire' Blanche is broken and ultimately violated and driven into madness. Marlon Brando's protrayal of the thug 'Stanley Kowalski' is one of the most terrifying protrayals I have even seen. Williams' play expresses for me my greatest fears about the cruelty of the world, which is why I react as powerfully to Laura, Blanche and Stanley. Interestingly, at the end of the play 'Desire' when Blanche is being led away her sister and neighbour comment on the blueness of the shawl she is wearing. Blanche tells them that the colour is Della Robbia blue – the blue mantle of Our Lady of Sorrows. The broken cry to Mary in their hour of sorrow. In this fleeting moment Williams catches this cry of the broken.

When one of Williams' plays *'The Rose Tattoo'*, was banned he complained that he was not advocating pornography or violence. He described himself as 'a surgeon of the Spirit' who analysed the violence that is in our soul and how we hurt one another. All the subjects Beckett and Williams expressed in their heart is the pain of lamenting, crying out for love in a world that bears so much rejection and violence. The psalms form a school of prayer. They capture all emotions – negative and positive and present them before God for his love and mercy. Rabbi Heschel called the psalms the birth pangs of theology. Dermot Cox saw them as forming a sacrament where our words bring us into the very presence of God. (*Psalms in the Life of God's People*, p 9). Walter Bruggermann in his work, *'The Message of the Psalms'* (pp 15-25) tells us that there is a movement, the psalms. Firstly, there are the psalms like Ps 1 which speak of the way we see things initially, then as we face the realities of life with its confusion we become disorientated (e.g. Ps. 55, 58, 88 etc) until finally we work to a new conclusion by grace in which we can praise God in a new way (e.g., Ps 146). It is a journey with the lonely Christ from Gethsemane to Calvary until we meet the dawn of Easter day – a journey we are on over and over again. Ps. 22 catches this movement of the psalms for me. It is the psalm of Jesus' passion (cf. Mk 15:55). Ps. 22 begins in the following way:

To the leader: according to The Deer of the
Dawn. A Psalm of David.

My God, my God, why have you
Forsaken me?

Why are you so far from

Helping me, from the
Words of my goaning?
O my God, I cry by day, but
You do not answer;
And by night, but find no rest.

Yet you are holy,
Enthroned on the praises of
Israel.
In you our ancestors trusted;
They trusted, and you
Delivered them.
To you they cried, and were
Saved;
In you they trusted, and were
Not put to shame.

But I am a worm, and not
Human;
Scorned by others, and
Despised by the people.
All who see me mock at me;
They make mouths at me, they
Shake their heads;
"Commit your cause to the

Lord; let him deliver –
Let him rescue the one in
Whom he delights!"

Yet it was you who took me
From the womb;
You kept me safe on my
Mother's breast.
On you I was cast from my
Birth,
And since my mother bore me
You have been my God.
Do not be far from me,
For trouble is near
And there is no one to help.

These verses consist of two complaints (vvi – 2, 6-8), each of which is followed by an expression of trust that looks to a better time, either in the life of the whole people (vv. 3-5) or in the psalmist's own life (vv. 9-10). This poignant alteration of complaint and trust seems only to make the psalmist's distress seem all the greater.

The psalm begins with the words 'My God' an address form that is rare and represents an especially intimate form of address based on a close personal relationship with God. (e.g. cf Ex. 15:2, Isa 44:17, Pss 63:1, 68:14 etc.). Now God seems to have forsaken his beloved and he cries out in anguish. He speaks in w. 3-5 of a time when God was close to his people.

However, he resumes his complaint in v. 6-8. The psalmist's experience of betrayal and rejection is utterly dehumanising. (cf. worm in Job 25:6; Isa 41:14). Apparent rejection leads to the psalmist's being scorned by others as well. The first section ends with a plea to God: "Do not be far from me, for trouble is near and there is no one else to help."

The imagery shifts in vv 12-21 to provide a terrifying description of the trouble:

Many bulls encircle me,
Strong bulls of Bashan
Surround me;
They open wide their mouths at
Me,
Like a ravening and roaring lion.

I am poured out like water,
And all my bones are out of
Joint;
My heart is like wax;
It is melted within my breast;
My mouth is dried up like a
Potsherd,
And my tongue sticks to my
Jaws;
You lay me in the dust of
Death.

For dogs are all around me;
A company of evildoers
Encircles me,
My hands and feet have
Shriveled;
I can count all my bones.
They stare and gloat over
Me;
They divide my clothes among

Themselves,
And for my clothing they cast
Lots.

But you, O Lord, do not be far
Away!
O my help, come quickly to
My aid!
Deliver my soul from the sword,
My life from the power of the
Dog!

Save me from the mouth of
The lion!

From the horns of the wild oxen
You have rescued me.

The animal imagery used by the psalmist is apparently used to represent powerful and abusive people (cf. Ps 7:2, Is 10:13, Jc 4:7 etc). In some ancient Near Eastern texts animals are used to represent demonic forces. This leads to the psalmist using anatomical features to show the nearness of death. The imagery indicates that the psalmist feels he is as good as dead. The final line of vv 19-21 is particularly important and it shows where the psalmist moves to meeting God whom he felt had deserted him. Clint McGann says the correct translation of the Hebrew text is "from the horns of the oxen you have answered me" (cf. NIB IV p. 763),

In short, the opening complaint has been reversed. God has answered. When the poet cried out in distress, 'My God, my God, why hast thou forsaken me' he has now found his answer. The answer comes not beyond the suffering, however, but precisely in the midst of and even from the suffering. God is present in the depths, even amid death. "In all our afflictions he was afflicted." (Isa 63:9).

Having found God in the pain and confusion the psalm ends with praise (v. 22-31).

I will tell of your name to my
brothers and sisters;
in the midst of the
congregation I will praise
you;
You who fear the Lord, praise
Him!
All you offspring of Jacob,
glorify him;
stand in awe of him, all you
offspring of Israel!
For he did not despise or abhor
the affliction of the afflicted;
he did not hide his face from
me,
but heard when I cried to
him.

From you comes my praise in
the great congregation;
my vows I will pay before
those who fear him.

The poor shall eat and be
satisfied;
those who seek him shall
praise the Lord.
May your hearts live forever.

All the ends of the heart shall
remember
and turn to the Lord;
and all the families of the nations
shall worship before him.
For dominion belongs to the
Lord,
and he rules over the nations.

To him, indeed, shall all who
sleep in the earth bow
down;
Before him shall bow all who
go down to the dust,
and I shall live for him.
Posterity will serve him;
future generations will be told
about the Lord,
and proclaim his deliverance to
a people yet unborn,
saying that he has done it.

There is an expression I once heard.   It said when one is
healed, the tribe is healed. We in our individualistic world
cannot really appreciate this. St. Seraphin of Sarov said
when one person finds peace a thousand are saved. The
healing brought by God to the psalmist brings others in to
the healing of God and this is what the last verses of the
psalm celebrate. The congregation joins the psalmist in
praising God (vv 22-23). The psalmist affirms that God is
with the afflicted and for this reason the people praise God.
To praise God's presence with the afflicted is to live. In vv.
27-31 the praise has universal effects reaching even the
land of the dead.

Ps. 22 relates in a special way to Jesus. It was his prayer on the cross. By telling the story of Jesus using Ps. 22 the Gospel writers affirm that in Jesus' faithful suffering God was present. God's presence with the afflicted and dying opens up new possibilities for living and understanding human life, as well as for understanding and accepting death. Jesus' cry on the cross (Matt. 27:46, Mk. 15:34) is not simply a cry of dereliction. It is an affirmation of faith in a God who, as the psalmists came to understand and articulate, shares human affliction. Entrusting one's life to this kind of God, as the psalmist and Jesus did, changes everything. In short love changes everything. Life can now be understood not as a frantic search for self-satisfaction and self-security, but as a life lived in dependence on God (cf. Matt. 6:25-33).

Jesus lived in this transformed *perspective*. He lived in humble dependence on God. He did not welcome suffering but embraced it on behalf of others. He faced death with the conviction that God's power is greater than death's power. All of this can be summarised in his words: "Not what I want, but what you want" (Mk. 14:36). Jesus lived like the psalmist, as one of the afflicted but in the knowledge that God does not despise the afflicted. (Ps. 22:24).

Rather God loves the afflicted and even shares their suffering. Jesus gathered around himself a community of the afflicted, the poor, the outcast. He sat at table with them and he still invites to his table those who prefer to live in humble dependence on God rather than on self. This is the table of the Eucharist.

In essence the Gospel writers recognised that Ps. 22 affirms what the life, death and resurrection of Jesus affirms. Suffering and glory are inseparable, both for the people of God and for God's own self.

Also it is in our brokeness and pain that we encounter

God and meet his healing love in Jesus.

This is not the only emotion the Psalmists meet head on. Anger is an emotion we as religious, and particularly male religious, have trouble dealing with or even acknowledging. This leads to resentment, bitterness and sometimes depression. It can also manifest itself in physical symptoms – small back pain, ulcers and heart conditions, coupled with blood pressure. The psalmist expresses his anger and negativity in the context of faith where he can be accepted and led to a constructive use for his anger.

The so-called cursing and imprecation psalms are something that are kept discreetly from view. In Ps58 the psalmist prays in the following way:

> *O God, break the teeth in their mouths;*
> *tear out the fangs of the young lions, O LORD!*
> *Let them vanish like water that runs away:*
> *like grass let them be trodden down and wither.*
> *Let them be like the snail that dissolves into slime;*
> *like the untimely birth that never sees the sun.*
> *Sooner than your pots can feel the heat of thorns,*
> *whether green or ablaze, may he sweep them away!*
> **(Ps 58: 6-9)**

Praying to God to break the teeth of those who hurt us seems strange to many of us. Ps 109 has the same note as this. Here the psalmist prays in the following way for the wicked one he despises:

> *When he is tried, let him be found guilty;*
> *Let his prayer be counted as sin,*
> *May his days be few;*
> *May another seize his position.*
> *May his children be orphans,*

And his wife a widow.
May his children wander about and beg;
May they be driven out of the ruins they inhabit.
May the creditor seize all that he has;
May strangers plunder the fruits of his toil.
May there be no one to do him a kindness,
Nor anyone to pity his orphaned children.
May his posterity be cut off;
May his name be blotted out in
The second generation.
May the iniquity of his father
Be remembered before the Lord.
And do not let the sin of his
Mother be blotted out.

(Ps 109: 7-14)

Ps. 137 was made very popular by the group Boney M, who recorded a single entitled *'By the Rivers of Babylon'.* It speaks of the episode where the captors ask the Israelites to sing one of Zion's songs. Yet in this version and also in such places as the Liturgy of the Hours the final verse is kept directly out of sight. It reads:

O daughter Babylon, you devastator!
Happy shall they be who pay you back
What you have done to us!
Happy shall they be who take your little ones
And dash them against the rock!

(Ps 137: 8-9)

These three psalms show that the psalmist is brutally honest about what some of us would have called 'unworthy feelings'. He brings his anger and desire for vengeance before God's loving kindness, acknowledging the reality of vengeful feelings in us. These psalms speak about the unfairness and exploitation that evoke rage.

There is an act of faith by which we can approach the presence of God whose rule is marked by faithfulness and compassion. Such rage is not only brought into *Yahweh's* presence, it is submitted to him and relinquished to him. Yahweh is one who takes the well-being of his people seriously. The raw speech of rage can be submitted to Yahweh because He will listen and act (Brueggemann, *Message of the Psalms*, p. 85). It is a safe place to own our emotions, negative as they may be and, in the light of acceptance, accept ourselves and in God's grace find constructive ways of dealing with anger. In union with God, anger can become a vehicle for change.

It is only in facing negativity that we grow and can allow grace enter. This enables us sing a new song of praise. Pss. 145-150 conclude the Psalter and are all psalms of praise. Ps. 145 begins with the following verses:

> I will extol you, my God and
> King,
> and bless your name forever
> and ever.
> Every day I will bless you,
> and praise your name forever
> and ever.
> Great is the Lord, and greatly to
> be praised;
> his greatness is unsearchable.

The psalmist can now praise God and he can say of God:

> The Lord is gracious and
> merciful,

slow to anger and abounding
in steadfast love.
The Lord is good to all,
and his compassion is over all
that he has made.

(Ps 145: 8-9)

In reaching out in pain, doubt, confusion and isolation the
psalmist has re-discovered God who is loving, tender and
compassionate. He concludes the psalm by showing how
God touched him and others in their pain:

The Lord is faithful in all his
Words,
And gracious in all his deeds.
The Lord upholds all that are
Bowed down.
The eyes of all look to you,
And you give them their food
In due season.
You open your hand,
Satisfying the desire of every
Living thing.
The Lord is just in all his ways,
And kind in all his doings.
The Lord is near to all who call
On him,
To all who call on him in truth.
He fulfills the desire of all whom
Fear him;
He also hears their cry, and
Saves them.
The Lord watches over all who
Love him,

But all the wicked he will
Destroy.

My mouth will speak the praise
Of the Lord,
And all flesh will bless his holy
Name forever and ever.

(Ps. 145: 14-21)

Here I remember Reinhold Schneider, a dramatist who
suffered from depression very much. He finds that he is
not alone in his suffering. He says:

'Shudder no longer before what is extraordinary
And look piously at the ultimate cruelties:
God suffers with you, you disappear into him.'
(see Von Balthasar, Tragedy Under Grace, p. 205)

The psalms of lament or 'disorientation' as Brueggemann
calls them find an echo in modern culture through the music
of U2. Bono wrote an introduction to a little work called,
'Selections from the Book of Psalms'. In it he tells of his
upbringing and how he learned to love the psalms. He saw
them not only as the roots of Gospel music, but also of the
'blues'. Abandonment, displacement is the very stuff of
his favourite psalms. It is in his despair that the psalmist
reveals the nature of his special relationship with God –
they are honest even to the point of rage. They prepared
Bono for the honesty of a John Lennon, the baroque
language of Bob Dylan. The poetry of the psalms opened
the way for him to the poetry of Ecclesiastes, the Song of
Solomon and the Gospel of John. For Bono, David was a
star, the Elvis of the Bible.

This influence permeates much of their music. In one of their most popular songs, they celebrate an Ecclesiastes mood like reflection on the Cross. They praise Jesus who takes on himself the cross of our sin and shame yet they remain struggling people seeking to find who they are and what their place in God's plan is.

They sing out:
I believe in the Kingdom Come
When all the colours will bleed into one,
But yes I'm still running.
You broke the bonds,
You loosed the chains,
You carried the cross and my shame;
You know I believe it.
But I still haven't found what I'm looking for.

It is a great song for all of us who seek to find who we are. It could also be someone seeking to find itself in a new world – all the time under the cross.

This album 'Pop' encapsulates very much the mood of the psalms of Lament. In one of the songs they cry out, 'Do you feel loved, do you feel loved?' It is a song of longing for love – a love that is often disappointed in life, like Laura in the *'Glass Menagerie'*. The mood of lament or complaint to God is caught in the song, 'If God Will Send his Angels':

"Hey, if God will send his angels,
And if God will send his angels
And if God will send his angels,
Would everything be alright.'

Then the voice of anguish, fear and disappointment is added:

"God has got his phone off the hook, babe, would he even pick it up if he could."

In the song *'Wake Up Dead Man'* they call out to Jesus who lies in the tomb. It is a cry of loneliness, isolation and near despair.

They say:

"Jesus, Jesus help me
I'm alone in the world
And a fucked up world it is too.
Tell me, tell me the story
The one about eternity
And the way its all gonna be
Wake up, wake up dead man."

It's a powerful Easter-Saturday type meditation when all seems lost and hope lies in the grave. The influence of the psalms can be seen here. In Ps 44:9-12 we read:

"You have rejected us and humiliated us.
You, our shepherd king, have made us sheep
For the slaughter.
You, our exodus liberator, have sold us
Cheaply into slavery."

(Ps 44: 9-12)

The call for the dead one to wake up echoes the call of the psalmist to God to come to us.

"Rouse yourself! Why do you sleep, O Lord,
Awake, do not cast us off forever!
Why do you hide your face?
Rise up, come to our help."

(Ps. 44: 23-24, 26)

"Pop" catches the mood of the psalms of lament or disorientation. Their 1999 *album 'All That You Can't Leave Behind'* catches the mood of psalms of praise or new orientation, the new Easter-day. The opening song is a song of joy 'Beautiful Day'. It puts one in mind of the day when God makes all things new – the resurrection of Jesus, a joy we are all called to. The impetus to live in Easter joy and new life is caught in the song 'Peace on Earth'. This song was written in the wake of the Omagh bombing. It shows an impatience to bring about a change of heart:

'Heaven on earth
we need it now
I'm sick of all of this hanging around
Sick of sorrow
Sick of pain
Sick of hearing again and again
That there's gonna be
Peace on earth.

It's in the last song in the album that we see this new peace on earth is not due to our own efforts alone. The last song is entitled 'Grace'. Bono in an interview he gave in 2001 muses over the fact that we hear and speak much of karma but so little of grace. Grace is the great treasure of the church. Uncreated grace is the Holy Spirit. Created grace is the effect of uncreated grace on the person. St. Paul in

Romans 5:5 speaks of the love of God poured out into our hearts by the Holy Spirit. This is the mystery of which U2 sing.

The words of the song go as follows:

Grace, she takes the blame
She covers the shame
Removes the stain
It could be her name.

Grace, it's the name for a girl
It's also a thought that changed the world.

What once was hurt
What once was friction
What left a mark
No longer stings
Because Grace makes beauty
Out of ugly things
Grace makes beauty out of ugly things.

The lament of "Pop" gives way to the grace of new life in the new album. Grace is the forgiveness of our sin, the healing of the past and leading us into a new vision of life where we work actively for peace. All our faults, failings in the light of the grace of God's love can be healed and transformed. "Grace makes beauty out of ugly things."

The album "All That you Can't Leave Behind" was delayed because Bono went to work for a time in an AIDS clinic in South Africa. There he saw the living reality of what he sang about in 'Grace'. He said of the people and place, "This is an amazing place, amazing people ... Our lives have been blessed by meeting you people today and I will never forget it." (*St Louis Dispatch*, May, 26th, 2002).

Grace can make all things new, bring beauty out of ugly things.

To Sing a New Song:

'Only love understands love'

The psalms of lament, Ecclesiastes, are among our most neglected resources but the 'Song of Songs' must be our most neglected. Over the centuries the allegorical interpretation became the only interpretation and some of the allegories took on a life of their own. Dermot Cox pointed out in his lectures the literal meaning of the Song is love poetry using sexual language and imagery. The Song originated in liturgical fragments from a fertility cult, wedding songs and love song after the manner of the Arabic Wasif – poems in praise of bodily beauty. The honesty and sense of joy comes as a shock to many of us who experienced a form of puritanical upbringing. Perhaps this is why the song is relegated to a secondary place. In the history of the Jewish people the Song enjoys an honoured place.

It belongs to a collection of scrolls called the 'Megilloth' which are used on the most sacred feasts. The Song is used at the Passover meal. It celebrates the saving power of God and the covenant of love he has made with his people and now renews in the feast. Human love helps us understand God's love. Simone Weil said to those who were shocked at the imagery of sexual love for divine love that if we did not allow this language then it would be like asking an artist to paint without paints.

Rabbi Akiba said that "… all the ages are not worth the day that the Song of Songs was given to Israel: all the writings are holy but the Song of Songs is the Holy of Holies' (cf. Joe Danby, *Mishnah*, p. 782). He favoured the allegorical interpretation but still keeping in mind the literal sense. Rilke, the poet, said that poetry can admit of many more meanings than the poet intended. Between the literal and the allegorical it's not a case of 'either-or' but a case of 'both – and'.

Love understands love and human love between two human beings throws light on another love, that of God. Both are holy. The poetry may not strike us at first because we are removed from the imagery of our time. Renita Weems in her commentary tells us that some of the expressions she heard today are far removed from any romantic language. She cites the expression, "My hormones are in warp speed for you" (NIB V, p. 395). Perhaps the language of the Song has something to offer!

The first poem is the voice of the woman. This is interesting in itself. It celebrates the freedom and sexuality of the woman – revolutionary for the times in itself. She says:

Bride: 'Let him kiss me with the kisses of his mouth
         Your love is more delightful than wine:
         Delicate in the fragrance of your perfume,
         Your name is oil poured out
         And that is why maidens love you.'

(1: 2-3)

She is longing for love. This longing is part of us and our lives. We all long deep down to be loved, appreciated and accepted. It is only in God that we find perfect love. St. John reminds us that God is love (Jn 4:8, 16).

Paul Tillich defines faith as the courage to accept acceptance. In the cross Tillich sees God as participating in our estrangement and its destructive consequences. St. Bernard says that the cross is God's statement: *"I love you"*.

So often our experience of life is negative and totally the opposite of love, we do not accept or find acceptance of love. Not to accept somebody is tantamount to killing them. When we are not accepted we find ourselves hostile and bitter, some indulge in inappropriate and unloving sexuality, others become pleasers, others become addicted to power, alcohol or any other forms that are available. Bernanos says, "Dear God! Why don't we realise more often that the mask of pleasure, stripped of all hyprocrisy, is precisly the mask of anguish?" (*Diary,* p. 140).

It is in Jesus if we can places ourselves as broken sinners around the cross at the sacrament of the eucharist which makes present the healing events of his life, death and resurrrection. The longing for life and celebration of that love are parts of prayer and that is why I list the Song of Songs in this chapter on prayer. The wedding feast and messianic banquet are frequent images for God's saving acts (cf. Hos 2:18-21, Ez 16,8, Is 62: 3-5 and Jn 2: 1-11) . Our happiness is God's concern.

St John of the Cross is regarded as the doctor of the nights of the soul. Many have shied away from his writings saying they are only for the 'special', the 'mystical' or 'strong'. In this way a major resource for prayer has been denied. Gerald G. May is a psychiatrist who is also trained in spirituality and theology.

In his work entitled *'The Dark Night of the Soul'* he shares some insights from John of the Cross. He sees the 'dark night' as taking different forms for different people. It can be addictions or depression. It can be trauma suffered from abuse by others. For John his own dark night included exile, imprisonment, starvation and abuse. It is when we are faced with our shadow side, our weaknesses and vulnerability and we are no longer in control. The 'dark night' is where we confront and attempt to integrate our weakness into becoming new people in God – the new creation. St. Therese of Lisieux in her delightful way of deconstructing received wisdom said in a letter to her sister that true sanctity consists in living with our imperfections patiently. (LT 243). It is in the dark night that under the transforming power of the living flame of love, we come to know God in our hearts.

The Song of Songs helps meditate on the weight of loneliness and loss. There are times when love is troubled by fear, doubt and lust. The bride doesn't respond to her beloved in time and she fears she will lose him so she sets off alone in the streets at night to find him (a daring move for a woman in that time). She says:

> Upon my bed by night
> I sought him whom my soul loves;
> I sought him, but found him not;
> I called him, but he gave no answer.
> "I will rise now and go about the city,
> in the streets and in the squares;
> I will seek him whom my soul loves."
> I sought him but found him not.
> The watchmen found me,
> As they went about in the city.
> "Have you seen him whom my soul loves?"
> Scarcely had I passed them,
> When I found him whom my soul loves.
>
> I held him, and would not let him go
> Until I had brought him to my mother's house,
> And into the chamber of her that conceived me.

(Sg 3: 1-4)

It is in bearing with ourselves patiently and placing ourselves before the transforming power of God in Jesus through the Spirit that we came to find love once more. It involves us admitting our weakness and vulnerability but all the time as broken sinners under the cross. At other places in the Song the tone is much more joyful and more full of fun, laughter and love. It is like the songs St. Francis so much loved. It is only after a long period of doubt and darkness we achieve peace.

It is because we are so afraid to face our darkness that so many live lives of quiet desperation. In the song the bride sings the following song when she re-discovers love in the beloved.

Bride: I hear my Beloved,
See how he comes
leaping on the moutains,
Bounding over the hills,
My Beloved is like a gazelle,
like a young stag.

See where he stands
behind our wall.
He looks in at the window,
He peers through the lattice.

My Beloved lifts up his voice,
He says to me,

'Come then, my love,
my lovely one, come.
For see, winter is past,
The rains are over and gone.
The flowers appear on the earth.

The season of glad songs has come,
the cooing of the turtledove is heard
in our land.
The fig tree is forming its first figs
and the blossoming vines give out their
fragrance.
Come then, my love,
my lovely one, come,
My dove, hiding in the clefts of the rock,
in the coverts of the cliff,
show me your face,
let me hear your voice;
for your voice is sweet
and your face is beautiful.'

(Sg 2: 8-14)

Taken as a whole the unit rhapsodizes the feeling of love that springs everywhere. The sight of sprinting animals (vv 8-9), the smell of figs and new buds (v.12) touch the heart and speak of new hope. With springtime comes belief in new adventure, new possibilities and a new outlook on life. The shepherd refers to this time of year as a time of singing (v.12) when the sound of turtledoves can be heard throughout the land. In the 'Mirror of Perfection' there is the story of how St. Francis could be overcome with a sense of joy when he beheld in the love of God revealed in Jesus. He would lift a stick from the ground and would draw across it with his right hand like a bow, as though he was playing a violin or some other stringed instrument. He would imitate the movements of the musician and sing in French. At other times he would weep over the memory of the suffering and death of Jesus. Life is a continual time of death and re-birth. There is the cross but there is also the new hope of the Easter dawn.

St. Francis' Prayer:

In the Fioretti the story of how Masseo asked Francis why the whole world followed after him (Ch 10). The Fioretti are stories that capture the spirit of Francis and his times rather than being factual accounts. His little story pushes the reader to see what made Francis special. The answer is manifold – a different one for each one who enters the story. For me the important part of Francis' life is summed up by Thomas of Celano when he says Francis not so much prayed as became prayer. (2 Cel 95). One of my own favourite accounts is when Francis began with his conversion and life of prayer. In 1 Cel 6 we read:

'Accordingly, he withdrew for a while from the bustle and the business of the world and tried to establish Jesus Christ dwelling within himself. Like a prudent businessman, he hid the treasure he had found from the eyes of the deluded, and, having sold all his possessions, he tried to buy it secretly. Now since there was a certain man in the city of Assisi whom he loved more than any other because he was of the same age at the other, and since the great familiarity of their mutual affection led him to share his secrets with him, he often took him to remote places, places well-suited for counsel, telling him that he had found a certain precious and great treasure. This one rejoiced and, concerned about what he heard, he willingly accompanied Francis whenever he was asked. There was a certain grotto near the city where they frequently went and talked about this treasure. The man of God, who was already holy by reason of his holy purpose, would enter the grotto, while his companion would wait for him outside; and filled with a new and singular spirit, he would pray to his Father in secret. He wanted no one to know what he did within, and taking the occasion of the good to wisely conceal the better, he took counsel with God alone concerning his holy proposal. He prayed devoutly that the eternal and true God would direct his way and teach him to do his will. He bore the greatest sufferings in mind and was not able to rest until he should have completed in deed what he had conceived in his heart; various thoughts succeeded one another and their importunity disturbed him greatly. He was afire within himself with a divine fire and he was not able to hide outwardly the ardor of his mind; he repented that he had sinned so grievously and had *offended the eyes of God's majesty,* and neither the past evils nor those present gave him any delight. Still he had not as yet won full confidence that he would be able to guard himself against them in the future. Consequently, when he came out again to his companion, he was so exhausted with the strain, that one person seemed to have entered, and another to have come out.'

Francis bore great sufferings in mind and spirit. In Gerald G. May's book entitled: *'The Awakened Heart'*, he tells the story of two people he was counselling. They complained of the feelings of unease in their lives and the longing that never seemed to be satisfied. He reminded them of Augustine's expression. 'You have made us for yourself O Lord and our hearts are restless until they rest in thee.' He pointed out to his two clients that they had swallowed the cultural myth that says, "If you are well-adjusted and living your life properly, you will feel fulfilled, satisfied, content and serene." Stated conversely, the myth says: "If you are not satisfied and fulfilled, there is something wrong with you." The truth is there is always a restlessness and emptiness in us. St. Francis had the courage to bear patiently with his emptiness and to wait on God.

'O Woman of the city,
Summer by they wild field doe
Not to wake or rouse us
Till we fulfill our love.'

(Sg. 3:5)

There is another aspect of this story that has always touched me. There is a companion to St. Francis who is a tower of strength. His quiet presence is often overlooked.

By his gentle support and listening he helped Francis remain sane and focussed. Meditating on him and on his quiet presence opened up the meaning of one of Alexander Solzhonitsgn's short stories: *'Matryona's House'*

This story is in many ways autobiographical. When Solzhenitsyn's was released from the Gulag, he was recovering from cancer of the throat. He felt lonely, broken and lost. He got a job away from Moscow teaching mathematics. An old lady named Matryona gave him lodgings.

She had known much tragedy in her life. She was a gentle person, supportive of Solzhenitsyn. He remarks that he never saw her pray, but late at night she would kneel down and pray before her icons when she thought no one could see her. In this atmosphere Solzhenitsyn began to heal mentally, spiritually and physically. Matryona died a tragic death and there was an unseemly family squabble afterwards. Solzhenitsyn ends his short story not there but with these words:

"None of us who lived close to her perceived that she was that one righteous person without whom, as the saying goes, no city can stand.
Nor the World."

(Matryona's House and Other Stories, p. 47)

CHAPTER IV: Prophets
God Meets Human Beings

Up to this we have concentrated on human beings calling out to God. Karl Barth speaks of the Bible as the place where the word of man and God meet. This is seen in the prophets. The author of the Letter to the Hebrews reminds us "… in various times and in various different ways God spoke to our ancestors through the prophets" (Heb 1:1). Then he goes on to tell us that in our time he speaks to us through his son Jesus. There is thus a continuity between the prophets and Jesus. When I studied the prophets first I found I was ill-served by the historical method. The origin and the history of the formation of the text did little to help me appreciate the depth and pathos of the prophets. The prophets were poets who spoke in the name of God. Walter Bruggeman in his work entitled *'Finally Comes the Poet'* shows us how these poets spoke to the hearts of kings and people and enflamed their hearts with a new vision. In George Orwell's work *'1984'* Winston Smith is tortured in room 101 to make him love Big Brother and abandon his independent thought. His torturer O'Brien tells him to continue the way he was going was "… pointless! Pointless!" However, O'Brien knows Winston's yearnings are not pointless. If he was let free he would be the one to inflame the spirit of the people, the 'proles'! That is why Big Brother is so afraid of Winston. The proles who make up 85 per cent of the population can be kept reasonably controlled. They love football, beer and pornography provided by Big Brother to keep them unaware and from thinking. On page 157 there is a significant saying: "By lack of understanding they remained sane".

The prophet does not allow this situation to remain. The people are challenged to see things anew and bring about change. The poet and the prophet are the most dangerous people. It was by reading Abraham Heschel's work entitled *'The Prophet'* that my eyes were opened. He was a holy man who, as his daughter Susannah said, lived as he wrote. He was inbued with the prophetic spirit. Paul Paul VI told clerical students from Milan that if they wanted to appreciate the prophets they should read Rabbi Heschel's work.

For Heschel, God takes instead the fate of individual human persons. The moral, spiritual and human state of humanity engage his attention. His care and concern for human beings are a central experience of the prophets (*'God in Search of Man'*, p. 21). The idea of *pathos* introduced by Hesehel denotes not simply an idea of goodness, but a dynamic, caring relationship between God and his people. The unfolding of biblical theology is the unfolding of God's love and care.

Pathos implies that the human predicament is also a divine predicament for God has a stake in the human situation. Sin is more than a failure for the individual because the human person is not just the image of God, but also the perpetual concern of God. The human creature is raised above the level of mere creature by the pathos of God and becomes "… a consort, a partner, a factor in the life of God" (The Prophet, p.7). God's concern and love for his people is something that is revealed to the prophets.

> To the prophet … God does not reveal himself in an abstract absoluteness, but in a personal and intimate relation to the world. He does not simply command and expect obedience. He is also moved and affected by what happens in the world, and reacts accordingly. ….
> Quite obviously in the biblical view, man's deeds may

move Him, affect Him, grieve Him or, on the other hand, gladden and please Him. This notion that God can be intimately affected, that He possesses not merely intelligence and will but also pathos, basically defines the prophetic consciousness of God.'

(Prophets, pp. 223-224)

For Heschel God is a lover engaged to his people, not only a king. "... God stands in a passionate relationship to human beings*" (Man is Not Alone,* p. 244). To have a passionate relationship with human beings is not only to be concerned for their welfare but to be moved and affected by their deeds and their plight. God is concerned to the point of being stirred by their doings and the condition in which they dwell.

What God said through the prophets he also says in a special way through his son, Jesus. From St. John Jesus is the word of God who reveals the Father (Jn. 1:1-18). This God is love (1 Jn 4:8, 16). It is God's love that lies at the base of Pathos. We human beings are created in the image of God so our feelings of suffering are analogous to divine pathos, but since God is greater than human categories ("... the apophatic way") his feelings, pathos are also different from our experience. Nonetheless our experience gives us insight into the divine concern, while still respecting the otherness of God. Hesehel tells us that the writings about the concern of God for his people are not crude anthropomorphisms, but profound understanding of God's love. God's love for human beings is eternal but the expression of that love is historical, depending on how we hear his voice and answer his call, whether we respond with love or callous indifference. Callous indifference is so often the response of humanity and this is what lies at the base of God's wrath expressed by the prophets.

For many individual petty acts of cruelty are a matter of some indifference. For God it is a disaster. This is what lies at the base of the prophets' cry for social justice for the widow, the orphan and the poor.

"God does not stand outside the range of human suffering and sorrow. His is personally involved in, even stirred by, the conduct and fate of man". (*Prophets*, p. 224). History is often the record of human misery and God is intimately concerned for human beings and involved in their history. We see this in the concern and care shown by Jesus even to the point of death. To have seen Jesus is to have seen the Father. (Jn 14:9).

The anguish of God echoes throughout the Bible. One example Heschel comments on is Isaiah 42:14: "… The allusion to the Lord as 'a woman in travail', the boldest figure used by any prophet conveys not only the sense of supreme urgency of His action, but also a sense of the deep intensity of his sufferings". Heschel also reminds us of God's involvement in human suffering when Isaiah proclaims courageously: "In all their afflictions he was afflicted". (Isaiah 63:9). God's pathos is a free response made intentionally by God. The pagan God, Moloch, requires the sacrifice of the life of man but the God of Israel hopes for the life of the human being. (*Man is Not Alone,* p. 45). In the Christian tradition Iraeneus says that the glory of God is a human being fully alive.

The prophets are those who see the world and its people with the eyes of God, *sub specie Dei*. They have glorified reality as reflected in God's mind. They have somehow experienced the pathos of God. God is involved in the life of his people. The prophet is an associate or partner of God, not just his mouthpiece. Heschel's analysis of the prophetic writings reveals that the fundamental experience of the prophet is a fellowship with the feelings of God.

It is a 'sympathy with the divine pathos', a oneness of consciousness which comes about through the prophets' participation with the divine pathos. In a sense the prophet lives the life of God. He hears God's voice and he feels God's heart. (*Prophets*, 14, 24-26). This is the basis for the fierce anger and intense indignation that so often flows through the prophetic writings. What to some may appear to be literary hyperbole – namely, the prophets raging against the mistreatment of the widow, against manipulation of the worker, against callousness and hardness against the poor – is in reality an attempt to express a profound sensitivity to the pathos of God. This profound sensitivity is in direct antithesis to the apathetic indifference so commonplace in the prophetic era, as it is today. Our age looks on acts of cheating in business or lying to one another or callousness to others as something slight, something that can easily be overlooked. To the prophets such acts are a disaster. Our age looks on simple injustices as passing episodes, scarcely noticeable. To the prophets these are catastrophic death blows to existence.

The "immoderate excitement" of the prophets, their excessive language, their violent outbursts are all traced by Heschel to their confrontation with the divine pathos which made them acutely aware of the "abysmal indifference to evil" which typifies their age as well as our own. What again appears to the casual reader as the gross exaggeration of the prophets is in reality a glimpse of God's concern for humanity. The prophet has become the voice that God bestows on the pain of the plundered poor, to the silent agony of a creation profaned by the powerful and wealthy. God has thrust a burden upon the prophet, the burden of his concern, of his vision and the prophet is bowed and stunned at the fierce greed he perceives. Behind the condemnation of the prophet lies the rage of God. (*Prophets*, 4-5). The prophet dreams the dream of God where callous indifference and cruelty are left behind and we find peace in God's presence. There is one beautiful paragraph that has always grabbed my attention. It has definite resonances in the Christian tradition with Jesus' Sermon on the Mount and Paul's account of the mystical body. (1 Cor 12). E.P. Sanders has shown in his various works such as *'Paul and Palestinian Judaism'* how profoundly Jewish was the world of Paul and how close he was to real rabbinic thought. Heschel says:

'Above all, the prophets remind us of the moral state of a people: few are guilty, but all are responsible. If we admit that the individual is in some measure conditioned or affected by that spirit of society, an individual's crime discloses society's corruption. In a community not indifferent to suffering, uncompromisingly impatient with cruelty and falsehood, continually concerned for God and every man, crime would be infrequent rather than common.'

(Prophets, p. 16)

I believe that this is true for all societies including the society of the church. Some abuse by clergy and religious asks serious questions about our society and way of life, power issues that have not been faced fully yet. All who are responsible show us that the society we create is also our own personal responsibility. When one hurts, we all hurt – the vocation of the prophet is to ease the pain. Paul tells us the same in 1 Cor 12:26, when one suffers we all suffer. Bonhoeffer, in his 'Letters and Papers from Prison' said that our vocation is to ease God's pain in the world. God's pain is the pain of his people. Heschel through the prophets points out that we all have a role in this healing. We are beloved of God but often cruelty, indifference or our own suffering have made some deaf to this voice for a time. Heschel knew this place of suffering, yet he gave himself over to God again. He says in another place:

> 'I am really a person who lives in anguish. I cannot forget what I have seen and have been through. Auschwitz and Hiroshima never leave my mind. Nothing can be the same after that. After all, we are convinced that we must take history seriously and that in history signs of the future are given to us. I see signs of a deterioration that has already begun. The war in Vietnam is a sign that we don't know how to live or how to respond. God is trying us very seriously. I wonder if we will pass the test? I am not a pessimist, because I believe that God loves us. But I also believe that we should not rely on God alone; we have to respond.'
>
> ### *(No Religion is an Island, p. 3)*

The prophet calls us to ease the blackout of God in all ages. Heschel says God has been expelled from many parts of our world to create a so-called earthly Paradise, which in reality has been no more than an extermination camp. God is reduced to being a mere slogan and his word is no longer spoken. (*Insecurity of Freedom,* p. 164-165). When this is done we become indifferent and do not see others as God sees them. We no longer dream his dream of a better world. Yet while '... The spiritual blackout is increasing daily, we no longer know how to resist the vulgar, how to say no in the name of a high yes. We have lost the sense of the holy. Our world is aflame with arrogant atrocities and naked violence. If not for my faith that God ... still listens to a cry, who could stand such agony?' (*On Prayer*, p. 11-12). In praying and living as we pray we begin to bring healing to God's pain in the world.

Hosea:

Hosea's prophecy dealt primarily with the Northern Kingdom of Israel and his favourite name for the land was Ephraim. Hosea was the prophet of the decline and fall of the Northern Kingdom and stood in the same relation to Ephraim in the eighth century as that in which Jeremiah stood a century and half later to Judah. He began his prophetic ministry in the prosperous days of Jeroboam 11 (786-746 B.C.) and lived through the period of anarchy which followed Jeroboam's death. He himself was married, the father of three children and well acquainted with agricultural life.

For many generations Israel and Judah were not disturbed by any power greater than the small countries around them. This came to an end in the middle of the ninth century when Assyria emerged as an empire and began to lead many expeditions across the Euphrates, compelling most of the state of Syria as well as the northern kingdom of Israel to submit to her sovereignty and pay tribute. These expeditions, nightmares of extreme ruthlessness, enriched Assyria with plunder of gold, silver and slaves. The history of the following two centuries is the story of the expansion of Assyria and later of Babylonia and the subjugation of western Asia. Tiglath-Pilser 111 (745-726 B.C.) was the emperor who oversaw the emergence of Assyria as an empire.

During the reign of Tiglath-Pilser the kingdom of Israel was in a state of anarchy. Within ten years following Jeroboam's death she had five kings, three of whom seized the throne in violence. In the reign of Menahem (795-738

B.C.) who had usurped the throne, Israel became a vassal of Assyria.

Menahem felt relatively secure under Assyria's protection. Yet the pro-Assyrian policy wreaked strong opposition. Menahem's son, Pekaliah (ca. 738-737 B.C.) was murdered by Pekal (737-732 B.C.), son of Remaliah who after taking over the rule of the kingdom and took place in the formation of an alliance between the smaller Asian state, directed against Assyria and hoping for support from Egypt. Hosea warned against the course Israel was heading in. He sends this warning:

> 'Ephraim shall become desolation
> In the day of punishment;
> Upon them I will pour out
> My wrath like water,
> Ephraim is oppressed, crushed in judgement, …
> Therefore, I am like a moth to Ephraim,
> And like dry rot to the house of Judah.'
>
> *(Hosea, 5:9-12)*

Political Promiscuity:

> 'O Ephraim, you have played the harlot,
> Israel is defiled.'
>
> *(Hosea 5:3; cf. 6:10; 9:1)*

At times Hosea used the term 'harlot' in a figurative sense, in the sense of political promiscuity. The kingdom was a ballad of plots and intrigues. When Menahem came to the throne by murder Hosea cried out: "A vulture is over the house of Israel!" (8:1).

For Hosea, there was no legitimate king in the country at all. Kingship was to be a divine institution but many of the kings emerged from violence and rebellion, the word proclaims:

"They made kings, but not through me,
They set up princes, but without my knowledge."

(Hosea, 8:4)

Nor was the competition found only in high places. All the people engaged in intrigues in one way or another:

All of them are hot as an oven,
And they devour their rulers,
All their kings have fallen;
And none of them calls upon Me.

(Hosea 7:7)

In addition to multiplying "falsehood and violence" (12:1) the various political factions, pro-Egyptian or pro-Assyrian, seeking to gain power or protection with the aid of foreign states, made the country a ready prey for the appetites of Assyria and Egypt.

Ephraim is like a dove,
Silly and without sense,
Calling to Egypt, going to Assyria, ...
They make a bargain with Assyria,
And oil is carried to Egypt.
(Hosea 7:11, 12:1 [H. 12:2]; cf. 8L12; 9:3, 6)

The political game of hiring allies among the nations was both perilous and blasphemous, with Israel lying between the mighty Assyrian empire and an ambitious Eygpt. Far from being a cure for Israel's weakness, taking advantage of the shifting political constellation could have had only the opposite effect.

For they saw the wind,
And they shall reap the whirlwind.
The standing grain has no heads,
It shall yield no meal;
If it were to yield,
Aliens would devour it,
Israel is swallowed up;
Already they are among the nations
As a useless vessel.

(Hosea, 8: 7-8)

In addition, an alliance with Assyria would have meant more than partnership in arms. It was Assyria's policy to require from her allies and tributaries recognition of her supreme god. Thus Israel was being led to the brink of the abyss.

Egypt, though not an abyss, could be like an earthquake. The central manifestation of the love and omnipotence of God, cherished and remembered in Israel, was the exodus from Egypt (11:1).

I am the Lord your God
From the land of Egypt;
You know no God but Me,
And besides Me there is no saviour.

(Hosea 13:4)

But reliance on Assyria and Egypt would end in exile rather than security.

They shall return to the land of Egypt,
And Assyria shall be their king,
Because they have refused to return to Me.
(Hosea 11:5; cf. 9:3, 6, 15; also 8:13)

Ephraim had given bitter provocation (12:14 [H. 12:15]); the judgement was inevitable and would not be long delayed. "Samaria shall bear her guilt, because she has rebelled against her God." (13:16 [H. 14:1]).

And yet the fall of Samaria was not the final phase in God's relationship to Israel. His love for Israel was ineradicable. He could not give up the people He loved (11:8). Hosea was sent primarily, not to announce doom, but to effect return and reconciliation.

Return, O Israel, to the Lord your God,
For you have stumbled because of your iniquity.
Take with your words
And return to the Lord;
Say to Him,
Take away all iniquity;
Accept that which is good,
Our lips will replace the offering of bullocks.
Assyria shall not save us,
We will not ride upon horses;
We will say no more,'Our God,'
To the work of our hands.
In Thee the orphan finds mercy.

The children of Israel shall return and seek the Lord their God, and David their King; and they shall come in fear to the Lord and to His goodness in the latter days.

I will be as the dew to Israel;
He shall blossom as the lily, ...
His shoots shall spread out;
His beauty shall be like the olive.
                    (Hosea 14:1-4, 3:5, 14:5-6)

Tension between Anger and Confusion:

What had Amos left undone, which Hosea must now do?
Amos had proclaimed the righteousness of God, His iron
will to let justice prevail. Hosea came to spell out the
astounding fact of God's love for man. God is not only the
Lord who demands justice; He is also a God Who is in love
with His people.

There is a tone of divine nostalgia for the early days of
God's relationship with Israel.

Like grapes in the wilderness,
I found Israel;
Like the first fruit on the fig tree,
In its first season
I saw your fathers.   ...
When Israel was a child, I loved him,
And out of Egypt I called My son.

(Hosea 9:10; 11:1)

Yet the more He called them, the more they went from
Him.

It was I Who taught Ephraim to walk,
I took them up in My arms;
But they did not know that I healed them.
I led them with cords of compassion,
With the bands of love;
I became to them as One Who eases the yoke on
their jaws,
I bent down to them and fed them gently.

(Hosea 11:3-4)

In the face of God's passionate love, the prophet is haunted by the scandal of Israel's desertion. "Israel has forgotten his Maker" (8:14). The voice of God's offended majesty fills his whole being.

She did not know
That it was I Who gave her
The grain, the wine, and the oil,
And Who lavished upon her silver
And gold which they used for Baal.

(Hosea 2:8 [H. 2:10])

She went after the Baalim "and forgot Me, says the Lord" (2:13 [H. 2:15]).

The fertility of nature is an astounding wonder. To the non-Hebrew population of Palestine, or Canaan, a land surrounded by desert, the mystery of growth, the marvel of spring, remained a perpetual surprise. There were powers behind all this – the local gods of the land, called the Baalim, who were regarded as the givers of wool and flax, of oil and wine, of grain, vines, and fig trees. (2:5, 12 [H. 2:7, 14]).

The conquest of Canaan by Israel was a process extending over several centuries. The Hebrews did not destroy the Canaanites. (cf. Ps. 106:34), but merely occupied parts of the land, while other parts remained in the hands of the Canaanites. For some time there was constant warfare between the two groups, but gradually hostilities ceased, and the Hebrews began to mingle.

... with the nations,
And learned to do as they did.
They served their idols,
Which became a snare to them.

They sacrificed their sons

And their daughters to the demons;
They poured out innocent blood,
The blood of their sons and daughters,
Whom they sacrificed to the idols of Canaan;
And the land was polluted with blood.
Thus they became unclean by their acts,
And played the harlot in the doings.
(Psalm 106: 35-39)

Without abandoning the cult of the God of their Fathers, the Hebrews worshipped the gods of the land they had conquered, sacrificing on the tops of the mountains and making offerings "upon the hills, under oak, poplar, and terebinth, because their shade is good" (4:13). The rites included sacred prostitution (4:14) as well as intoxication. It was the worship of a god of the land rather than of the Creator of heaven and earth; a god who in return for the blessings of fertility demanded the gifts of incense and the excitements of the flesh rather than a God Who in return for all blessings demanded righteousness and justice, love and mercy, faithfulness and attachment, Who was the Lord of nature everywhere as well as the Master of history at all times.

"They... make for themselves molten images: and sacrifice to them (13:2 f). They do not realise their stupidity. "Men kiss calves" (13:2). "A people without understanding shall come to ruin" (4:14).

My people are destroyed for lack of knowledge;
Because you have rejected knowledge,
I reject you from being a priest to Me.
(Hosea 4:6)

100

The serenity of the people, who felt safe in the enthusiastic worship of both God and the Baalim, was shattered by the prophet, whose words fell like the blows of a hammer over their heads:

I am the Lord your God
From the land of Egypt;
You know no God but Me,
And besides Me there is no saviour.
It was I who knew you in the wilderness,
In the land of drought;
But when they had fed to the full,
They were filled, and their heart was lifted up;
Therefore they forgot Me.
So I will be to them like a lion,
Like a leopard I will lurk beside the way.
I will fall upon them like a bear robbed of her cubs,
I will tear open their breast,
And there I will devour them like a lion,
As a wild beast would rend them.

(Hosea 13:4-8)

How deeply Hosea must have sensed the pathos of God to have been able to convey such dreadful words against his own people whom he loved so deeply. These words, however, were neither a final judgement nor an actual prediction. Their true intention was to impart the intensity of divine anger. And yet that anger did not express all that God felt about the people. Intense is His anger, but profound is His compassion. It is as if there were a dramatic tension in God.

Hosea expressed solidarity with the pathos of God who saw his people move away from him into violence, injustice and their ultimate destruction. However, the reality is that

Israel is erratic and her love is fleeting. God's expression comes to compassion in the words of Hosea:

> *'... What shall I do with you, O Ephraim?*
> *What shall I do with you, O Judah?*
> *Your love is like a morning cloud,*
> *Like the dew that goes early away.*
> *Therefore, I have hewn them by the prophets,*
> *I have slain them by the words of my mouth....'*
>
> *(Hosea 6:4-5)*

Hosea sees a Drama:

Amos knows God as the selfless and exalted Being whose sensibilities and concern for justice are pained by the sinful transgressions of Israel. Hosea glimpses the inner life of God as he ponders his relationship to Israel. In parables and in lyrical outbursts the decisive motive behind God's strategy in history is declared. The decisive motive is love.

God is the One who is always loving but is the one to whom deception comes but continues to plead for loyalty and uttering a longing for reunion, and a passionate desire for reconciliation. At the beginning "... when Israel was a child, I loved him" (11:1). Hosea is able to express as prophet the love of God for Israel in all its most varied forms – as compassion (11:8), as a mother's tenderness (1:6-8, 2:3, 6, 21, 25; 11:1) and as love between husband and wife (3:1ff). From the perspective of the fundamental disposition of love it is understandable that healing and reconciliation, not harm and destruction, finally prevail. Hosea's emotional solidarity with God is apparent throughout the book.

Hosea's conception of Israel as the consort of God represents one of the most original ideas in the history of

Judaism (cf. Isa 49:14, 15; 62:5) and foreshadow the traditional interpretation of the Song of Songs. In God's love for Israel He has a passionate love of right and hatred of evil. This explains the vehemence of the angry passages of Hosea. It is where God calls his people to leave wickedness, callousness and indifference behind. It is the utterance of pathos – not a decree, not a decision.

Behind all this is God's hope that Israel will come back to him. He hopes for the day when:

> "… you will call Me 'my husband', … and I will betroth you to Me for ever; I will betroth you to Me in righteousness and in justice, in love and in mercy. I will betroth you to Me in faithfulness, and you shall know the Lord" (2:16, 19-20 [H. 2:18, 21-22]). The reconciliation will take effect as a new betrothal. And these will be the gift and dowry for the bride: righteousness, justice, kindness, mercy. The pathos of love, expressed first in the bitterness of disillusionment, finds its climax in the hope of reconciliation. "I will heal their backsliding, I will love them freely, for Mine anger has turned from him"
>
> *(14:4 [H. 14:5])*

Rabbi Heschel suggests a reason why Hosea can see so deeply into the pathos of God. He refers to the strange narration of Hosea's marriage to Gomer. According to the Book of Hosea they were happy in their mutual affection. Three children were born, to whom Hosea gave symbolic names. Subsequently however, he discovered that Gomer had been unfaithful. For Heschel the marriage of Hosea was no symbolic representation of real facts. The message behind the prophet's statement is the prophet's experience of a broken relationship with his wife and the breakup of his marriage. As time went by, Hosea became aware of the part that his personal fate was a mirror of the divine pathos, that his sorrow echoed the sorrow of God. (*Prophets*, p 56).

Daath Elohim:

Hosea's central complaint against the people is that they do not know God. He employs the verb "to know" with striking frequency and coins the expression *daath Elohim*, usually rendered as "knowledge of God". The verb "yad" does not mean simply "to know", "to be acquainted with". In most Semitic languages it signifies sexual union as well as mutual and spiritual activity. In Hebrew 'yada' means more than the possession of abstract concept. It means profound and deep union, an inner feeling for and a reception into the soul. (*Prophets*, p.57). It includes concern, inner engagement, dedication and attachment to a person. In the Book of Exodus God hears the peoples' cry and "God knew their condition" (Ex. 2:25). What the text means is that God has sympathy for and is affected by the people's plight. Israel is later told not to oppress the stranger for "… you know the heart of a stranger, for you were strangers in the land of Egypt" (Ex. 23:9). You have empathy with, or a feeling for the heart of a stranger.

The relationship between God and Israel, as conceived by Hosea in terms of marital love, desertion and the hope for a new betrothal, calls not only for right action, but also for a feeling of love for each other on the parts of those involved. The words *daath Elohim* means sympathy for love, attachment to the whole person, his love as well as his knowledge. It is an act of attachment to God. The biblical man knew of no bifurcation of mind, heart and emotion. He saw the whole person in a human situation.

"For I desire steadfast love and not sacrifice, daath of God, rather than burnt offerings" (6:6); *daath* corresponds to *hesed*, or love. What is desired is an inner identification with God rather than a mere dedication to ceremonies.

Thus the expression *daath elohim* must be understood in the framework of Hosea's thinking of the God-Israel relationship as one of engagement, marriage, betrayal, and remarriage.

> Their deeds do not permit them
> To return to their God.
> For the spirit of harlotry is within them
> And they know not the Lord. ...
> They have dealt faithlessly with the Lord,
> For they have borne alien children.
>
> *(Hosea 5:4, 7)*

As an antithesis to "the spirit of harlotry", knowledge of God must mean an intimate relation to, or a feeling for, God.

According to the analogy of sexual union to which this verb points, this sympathy must be understood to imply an emotional experience that is reciprocal. Just as in sexual reciprocal emotion, where the feeling of one person is in no sense an object to the other, where rather both persons share the same feeling, the structure of the sympathy implied in Hosea's hypothesis is not compassion for one another, but a suffering together, the act of sharing an inner experience.

The word, then, as we have seen, has an intellectual as well as an emotional meaning. In most passages, the intellectual component of *daath* is stressed; in Hosea, the emotional component seems to be primary. His daath elohim does not constitute a knowledge of God, but an awareness of God, a sensitivity of what concerns him – in short, a loving union with the Beloved.

That the word daath in Hosea denotes an act involving complete engagement of the person may be inferred from the words in which God predicts the new relationship with his people (2:19-20 [H. 2:21-22]). Personal involvement, like the one that occurs when a man becomes engaged to a woman, seems to be regarded as the prerequisite for, or the essence of, the daath or "knowledge" of God. "I am the Lord your God from the land of Egypt; ... It was I who knew you in the wilderness, in the land of drought" (13:4-5). What the prophet means is "I *cared* for you" or "I was *attached to* you".

Unlike the prophetic sympathy, which arises in response to a revelation and the pathos it discloses, the general sympathy which Hosea requires of man is a constant solidarity; an emotional identification with God. It is the central religious postulate. The loss of daath is the cause of man's undoing (4:6).

The contrast between Amos and Hosea is seen both in what they condemn and in what they stress. To Amos, the principal sin is *injustice;* to Hosea, it is *idolatry.* Amos inveighs against evil deeds; Hosea attacks the absence of inwardness. In the words of Amos:

> I hate, I despise your feasts, ...
> I will not accept your sacrifices. ...
> But let justice roll down like waters,
> And righteousness like a mighty stream.
>
> *(Amos 5: 21-24)*

In the words of Hosea:

For I desire love (hesed) and *not sacrifice,*
Attachment to God *rather than burnt offerings.*

(Hosea, 6:6)

In surveying the past, Amos dwells on what God has done
(2:9 ff); Hosea dwells on what God has felt for Israel
(11:1-4). *"You only have I known of all the families of
the earth,"* in the words of Amos (3:2). *"When Israel
was a child, I loved him",* in the words of Hosea (11:1).
And again from Hosea: *"There is no loyalty ('emeth), no
love (hesed), and no knowledge of God in the land".*
(4:1)

Deutero – Isaiah:

Charles R. Seitz in his commentary on the record part of
the Book of Isaiah (NIB VI, pp 307-563) presents chapters
40-66 as forming a unitary literary whole. The final redactor
has welded what we once called Deutero-Isaiah and Trito
Isaiah in to one coherent whole. Rabbi Heschel, too, sees
chapters 46-66 as forming one book. I am convinced by
the arguments.

Background to Deutero-Isaiah:

The Neo-Babylonian empire did not last long. It declined
rapidly after the death of Nebuchadnezzar in the year
562B.C.E. Cyrus, the Persian king of the little principality
of Elam, succeeded in overpowering the two powers that
had divided the Near Eastern world at the fall of Assyria.
He defeated the King of the Median Empire in 550 and the
King of Babylonia in 539. Cyrus was now the head of the
great Persian Empire, and his power extended as far as
the western coast of Asia Minor.

It was in this exciting period that a prophet arose who lifted the meaning of these events from the level of political history to the level of understanding world history as a drama of redemption.

He proclaimed that the Lord was about to redeem His people, that Babylon would fall, and that Cyrus, who had been called and empowered by the Lord to carry out His will in history (41:5:7; 44:28; 45:1 f), was destined to play an important part in the return of Israel to Zion and in the restoration of Jerusalem.

The majestic words of this prophet, whose name is unknown, are found in the later chapters of the book of Isaiah (chs. 40-66). The message of Second Isaiah as he is conventionally called, is of no age. It is prophecy tempered with human tears, mixed with a joy that heals all scars, clearing a way for understanding the future in spite of the present.

No words have ever gone further in offering comfort when the sick world cries.

(Prophets, p. 145)

Jeremiah, followed by the Book of Lamentations, shows the state of the sick world as it collapsed before Deutero-Isaiah came to be smitten during the Babylonian captivity. The prophet Jeremiah bore the cry of a sick world before the fall of Jerusalem and Judah in 587 B.C. when Jerusalem and the temple was destroyed and the people led off into Babylonian captivity. He felt heavily the weight of suffering, the pathos of God and the rejection and arrogance of the people, its prophets and leaders. He poured out his heart in lament to God.

In Jer 12: 1-2, Jeremiah faces his bitter experience and turns to God and complains:

> *You will be in the right,*
> *O LORD,*
> *When I lay charges against you;*
> *But let me put my case to you.*
> *Why does the way of the guilty prosper?*
> *Why do all who are*
> *Treacherous thrive?*
> *You plant them, and they take root;*
> *They grow and bring forth fruit;*
> *You are near in their mouths*
> *Yet far from their hearts.*

Jeremiah sets out this complaint in a legal form, as if he is trying to bring God to trial. His charge is that the guilty prosper and the treacherous thrive. They use the name of God but they are far from him in their hearts. Yet the one who suffers is Jeremiah.

In 20:14-18, we see Jeremiah still in the grip of the same mood of deep personal despondency. The dark shadow of failure and rejection has blighted his life.

The curse he shouts out here is much more violent than any found in the psalms of lament:

> Cursed be the day
> on which I was born!
> The day when my mother bore me
> let it not be blessed!
> Cursed be the man
> who brought the news to my father, saying,
> 'A child is born to you, a son,'
> making him very glad.

Let that man be like the cities
that the LORD overthrew
without pity;
let him hear a cry in the morning
and an alarm at noon.
because he did not kill me in the womb;
so my mother would have
been my grave,
and her womb forever great;
Why did I come forth from the womb
to see toil and sorrow,
and spend my days in shame?

(Jer 20: 14-18)

This 'before-birth-death-wish' is very uncharacteristic of the Old Testament. Life comes as God's gift, a gift to be enjoyed and lived to the full. Even the author of Ps22 in the dark nights of his soul, surrounded by rejection, scorn and abuse, draws strength from remembering:

'Yet it was you who took me
from the womb;
You have kept me safe on my
Mother's breast
On you I was cast from my birth,
And since my mother bore me
You have been my God.'

(Ps 22: 9-10)

The only parallel to Jeremiah's cry is to be found in Job 3, which may have been influenced by Jeremiah's words. The spirit of these words is a wish to have never been. He is lonely, feels abused and that all he does is a waste. Life had become a burden too heavy to bear. Jeremiah cries out:

> *'Why is my pain unceasing,*
> *my wound incurable,*
> *refusing to heal?'*

The most shocking of Jeremiah's reproaches and complaints is against God and is found in 20: 7-8. He lashes out, saying:

> *"You have seduced me, Yahweh,*
> *And I have let myself be seduced;*
> *You have overpowered me:*
> *You were the stronger.*
> *I am a laughing stock all day long*
> *They all make fun of me"*

The Book of Lamentations was written after Jeremiah's prophecies when the old world had now totally collapsed and the end of the book cries to Yahweh from where there seems to be no reply. It is in the light of these that the true hope of Deutero-Isaiah can be seen.

New Hope:

The book begins with the following message:

> 'Console my people, console them'
> says your God
> 'Speak to the heart of Jerusalem
> and call to her
> and her time of service is ended,

that her sin is atoned for,
that she has received from the land of Yahweh
double punishment for all her crimes.'

A voice cries, 'Prepare in the wilderness
a way for Yahweh,
Make a straight highway for our God
across the desert,
let every valley be filled in,
every mountain and hill be laid low,
let every cliff become a plain,
and the ridges a valley;
then the glory of Yahweh shall be revealed
and all mankind shall see it;
for the mouth of Yahweh has spoken.'
A voice commands: 'Cry!'
and I answered, 'What shall I cry?'
-'All flesh is grass
and its beauty like the wild flowers.
The grass withers, the flower fades
when the breath of Yahweh blows on them.
(The grass is without doubt the people)
The grass withers, the flower fades,
but the word of our God remains for ever.'

(Isa 40: 1-8)

This oracle is the voice of Yahweh who breaks the silence
of exile and by utterance transforms the hopes of a people
who were rejected and almost in despair. Yahweh is
preparing a new exodus of his people from the land of
despair to new hope. Frederich Bueckner relates this hope
to a personal level. He asserts: "No matter how much the
world shatters us to pieces, we carry inside us a vision of
wholeness that we sense is our true home and that beckons

us" (*The Longing for Home*, p. 110).   Similar oracles of comfort are found throughout the pages of Deutero-Isaiah. We read:

> But now, thus says Yahweh,
> Who created you, Jacob,
> Who formed you, Israel:
> Do not be afraid, for I have redeemed you;
> I have called you by your name, you are mine.
> Should you pass through the sea, I will be with you;
> Or through rivers, they will not swallow you up.
> Should you walk through fire, you will not be scorched
> and the flames will not burn you.
> For I am Yahweh, your God,
> the Holy One of Israel, your saviour.
>
> I give Egypt for your ransom,
> and exchange Cush and Seba for you.
> Because you are precious in my eyes,
> because you are honoured and I love you,
> I give men in exchange for you,
> peoples in return for your life.
> Do not be afraid, for I am with you.
>
> *(Isa 43: 1-9)*

and later:

> For Zion was saying: 'Yahweh has abandoned me,
> The Lord has forgotten me'.
> Does a woman forget her baby at the breast,
> or fail to cherish the son of her womb?
> Yet even if these forget,
> I will never forget you.

See, I have branded you on the palms of my hands;
Your ramparts are always under my eye.
Your rebuilders make haste,
and your destroyers and despoilers depart.

(Isa 49: 14-15)

On the historical level it is through Cyrus that the Babylonian empire collapses but the action of Yahweh is realised in a mysterious way. He is present to the people and it is the suffering servant who mediates this presence. The servant is one who reverses the sinful ways of those who reject God – he is one who lives God's will and surrenders himself into God's hands. Controversy has raged throughout the centuries as to the identity of this servant – I will come to this in a moment.

In the earlier servant songs Israel seems to be the one addressed (42: 1-4, 49: 1-6) but in the later songs it seems to be an individual who lives in himself the call of the servant for Israel. In 50: 4-9, we read:

The Lord Yahweh has given me
a disciple's tongue,
So that I may know how to reply to the wearied
he provides me with speech,
Each morning he wakes me to hear,
to listen like a disciple.
The Lord Yahweh has opened my ear.

For my part, I made no resistance,
neither did I turn away.
I offered my back to those who struck me,
my cheeks to those who tore at my beard;
I did not cover my face
against insult and spittle.

114

The Lord Yahweh comes to my help,
so that I am untouched by the insults,
So, too, I set my face like flint;
I know I shall not be shamed.

My vindicator is here at hand.
Does anyone start proceedings against me?
Then let us go to court together.
Who thinks he has a case against me?
Let him approach me.

The Lord Yahweh is coming to my help,
who dare condemn me?
They shall all go to pieces like a garment
devoured by moths.

It is through this mysterious suffering servant that Yahweh brings about the healing of the division between him and his people.

It is through him that the message of comfort is being realised. Those standing by are urged to become servants of the servant.

Let anyone who fears Yahweh among you
listen to the voice of his servant!
Whoever walks in darkness,
and has no light shining for him,
let him trust in the name of Yahweh,
let him lean on his God.

(Is. 50:10)

It is in the fourth servant song that the full vocation of the suffering servant is given. In trying to understand this I am indebted to the viewpoints of Martin Buber and Walter

Bruggemann to whose works I now turn:

Martin Buber in his work *The Prophetic Faith*, argues that throughout history there appear to be people who embrace the vocation spoken about in this poem.

One man he had in mind was his friend Franz Rosenweig, who was very ill towards the end of his life, though he still collaborated with Buber in the German translation of the Hebrew Bible. While he suffered, those around him found themselves enriched by his presence. For me as a Christian, Jesus embodies the suffering servant vocation in a radical way, as the Son of God.

The songs of the Servants are a poetic vehicle and allow, as Rilke said, many diverse interpretations – the form of the servant can take different forms at different times. The poem of the suffering servant begins:

See, my servant shall prosper;
He shall be exalted and lifted up,
And shall be very high.

(Isa 52:13)

For this section I use Walter Brueggemann's translation of the suffering-servant poem (cf. *Isaiah 40-66*, p. 141-150). The opening line voices the ultimate resolve of Yahweh that the servant (whoever he may be) will be honoured in the end and exalted. The opening verse is matched by the concluding assertion about the exultation of the servant. (53: 10-12).

Just as there were many who were astonished at him
-so marred was his appearance, beyond human semblance,
and his form beyond that of mortals –
so he shall startle many nations;

116

Kings shall shut their mouths because of him;
For that which has not been told them they shall see,
and that which they had not heard they shall contemplate.

(52: 14-15)

Verse 14 portrays the servant as a marked, distorted figure. He is not one of the beautiful people. He is a rather disfigured person upon whom one can hardly bear to look. This sorry portrayal is abruptly countered in verse 15 by the assertion that nations and kings are awed by the servant and assume a respectful silence before this mysterious one. The humiliated one becomes the exalted one in whom Yahweh works.

The poem must be understood in the context of the Isaiah tradition. Therefore as the servant is Israel (a common assumption of Jewish interpretation) we see that the theme of humiliation and exaltation serves the Isaiah rendering of Israel, for Israel in tradition is the humiliated (exalted) people of Israel, who by the powerful intervention of *Yahweh* is about to become the exalted restored people of Zion. This drama of Israel is the first subject of the poetry. As a Christian I see the servant relived in the figure of Jesus in a unique way. He is the very son of God. In the passage from St. Paul, *Philippians 2:5-22*, it says of Jesus:

Who, though he was in the
form of God,
did not regard equality with
God
as something to be exploited,
But emptied himself,
taking the form of a slave,
being born in human likeness.
And being found in human form,

117

he humbled himself
and became obedient to the
point of death –
even death on a cross.
Therefore God also highly
Exalted him
And gave him the name
That is above every name,
So that at the name of Jesus
Every knee should bend,
In heaven and on earth and
Under the earth,
And every tongue should confess
That Jesus Christ is Lord,
To the glory of God the Father.

(Phil 2: 6-11)

Here we see the theme of humiliation in the death of Jesus and the theme of exaltation as God raises him from the dead. The poem of the suffering servant is important for understanding Jesus. Also in Acts 8 where Philip interprets this part of Isaiah as referring to Jesus.

Walter Brueggemann reminds us that the Jewish conviction of Israel going from exilic humiliation to restored exultation and the Christian conviction of Jesus being humiliated in crucifixion and exalted at Easter have for a long time been in deep tension. Brueggemann's own judgement is that it is more important to recognise the communality and parallel structure of Jewish and Christian claims at the core of faith (p. 143). Isa 52: 13 – 52:12 is a poem and does not permit one single solution. Rilke speaks of someone reading a poem and realising many more meanings than the poet intended. Here there is room for both interpretations and, following Buber's lead, we can see the poem realised in the hearts of others too, in the course of history.

The example of Franz Rosenweig in his last years once again comes to mind. For me as a Christian the realisation of the suffering servant vocation in Jesus is important. As son of God he lived this in a special way.

> Who has believed what we have heard?
> And to whom has the arm of the Lord been revealed?
> *(53:1)*

This passage bears witness not only to the power of Yahweh and the destiny of the servant, but also to the faith of the community that experiences healing from the suffering one.

> For he grew up before him like a young plant,
> And like a root out of dry ground;
> He had no form or majesty that we should look at him,
> Nothing in his appearance that we should desire him.
> He was despised and rejected by others;
> A man of suffering and acquainted with infirmity;
> And as one from whom others hide their faces
> He was despised, and we held him of no account.
> *(53: 2-3)*

The servant was a rejected person, perhaps ostracised, perhaps disabled, of whom nothing was expected. He was not one of the great ones on the earth.

> Surely he has borne our infirmities
> And carried our diseases;
> Yet we accounted him stricken,
> Struck down, and afflicted.
> But he was wounded for our transgressions,

119

Crushed for our iniquities;
Upon him was the punishment that made us whole,
And by his bruises we are healed.
All we like sheep have gone astray;
We have all turned to our own way,
And the LORD had laid on him the iniquity of us all.

(vv 4-6)

This very one took on himself disabilities and diseases, all caused by sin. By accepting all this, the servant was crushed, wounded and broken. Yet we are the ones who are healed. In Isa 63:9 we have the line speaking of Yahweh: 'In all our afflictions he was afflicted.' All our sufferings are God's and we see this in Jesus in a special way who took on himself the wounds of sin and disease to the point of his breakdown and death. The servant is one who is in sympathy with Yahweh, and who has compassion for the people.

By acting the role of servant he brings healing to a broken relationship. In the poem on the work of the servant we find a section that is dominated by first person-pronouns; 'me, our, us etc'. This is not a cold detached statement. It is rather our voice of hope, poured out in passionate, personal terms.

He was oppressed, and he was afflicted,
Yet he did not open his mouth;
Like a lamb that is led to the slaughter,
And like a sheep that before its shearers is silent,
So he did not open his mouth.

By a perversion of justice he was taken away.
Who could have imagined his future?
For he was cut off from the land of the living,

120

Stricken for the transgression of my people.
They made his grave with the wicked
And his tomb with the rich,
Although he had done no violence.

The servant was oppressed, afflicted and done in by a 'perversion of justice'. He was not guilty and thus should have received no punishment. He is the righteous sufferer we have met in the psalms and in Job. In the Gospel of John Jesus is referred to as 'the lamb of God who takes away the sin of the world; (John, 1:29). His is a life given for others – no satisfaction of anger, a giving of oneself to the point of death. He did this so we could realise that all pain and rejection die with him and when he rises again he gives us new life. My sufferings are his. I am on a journey from Gethsemene to Calvary.

The final section of the suffering-servant poem reads:

Yet is was the will of the LORD to crush him with pain.
When you make his life an offering for sin,
He shall see his offspring, and shall prolong his days;
Through him the will of the LORD shall prosper.
Out of his anguish he shall see light;
He shall find satisfaction through his knowledge,
The righteous one, my servant, shall make many righteous,
And he shall bear their iniquities.
Therefore, I will allot him a portion with the great,
And he shall divide the spoil with the strong;
Because he poured out himself to death,
And was numbered with the transgressors;

Yet he bore the sin of many,
And made intercession for the transgressors.

(vv 10-12)

In verse 9 we seemed to have arrived at the end of the poem, yet it continues with the phrase 'Yet Yahweh' (v10). It is Yahweh, God, who insists the poem continues. The servant gave all and our God makes him receive all.

In verses 11b – 12 the words are on the lips of Yahweh. The servant makes righteous those who are judged. Therefore, God exalts the servant. The servant is one who stood in the midst of the afflicted and the sinful and now he is exalted. Some think the poem speaks of the resurrection. However, this is not said, rather it is said that Yahweh exalts the servant. However, it certainly prepares the ground for the resurrection to take root in the hearts of the people. His life is fulfilled in the resurrection of Jesus from the dead. Jesus in his mission as a suffering servant shows us the depths to which God will go so that we may know we are loved and beloved of him. The remainder of the work is the reply of the servants of the Servant who with their healing hand brings the light of Yahweh to the earth.

Servants of the Servant:

The servant song was very important in the early church for understanding the apparent failure of the Cross and Calvary. Those who meditated on the Cross and resurrection became servants of the Servant.   I now turn my thoughts to just a few of these.

(a) Paul: In his letter to the Phillipines in his great hymn (2:5-11), Paul shows how he saw Jesus as the new suffering servant of Yahweh. Later he meditates and draws life through the Spirit of Jesus. He says:

> Yet whatever gains I had, these I have come to regard as loss because of Christ,
> More than that, I regard everything as loss because of the surpassing value of knowing Christ Jesus my Lord. For his sake I have suffered the things, and I regard them as rubbish, in order that I may gain Christ, and be found in him, not having a righteousness of my own that comes from the law, but one that comes through faith.
>
> I want to know Christ and the power of his Resurrection and the sharing of his sufferings by Becoming like him in his death,
> If somehow I may attain the resurrection from the dead.
>
> *(Phil 3: 7-11)*

He wants to know Christ in all the power of his resurrection. In the way he embraces whatever comes and turns it over to God's transforming power. In this is his joy. In the second letter to the Corinthinans we see how Paul actually did this. In 2 Cor 1:8 there is a little line that is often passed over. He tells us, his Corinthian audience: "For we would like you to realise, brothers, that the things we had to undergo in Asia were more of a burden than we could carry, so that we despaired of coming through alive" (1:8)[1]. Paul knows the meaning of failure and near-despair. This moment was a turning point in Paul's life.

---

[1] For this section I am endebted to the work of A.E. Harvey, *'Renewal Through Suffering'* (Edinburg: T.T. Clark, 1996)

The whole tone in 2 Corinthians and the later correspondence becomes more human and understanding than what we knew formerly of Paul. In Acts 15 we hear how Barrabas and Paul parted after a violent quarrel.

Paul survived his moment of despair and it was in the light of this that he gave the following blessing:

Blessed be the God and Father of our Lord Jesus Christ, a gentle Father and the God of all consolation, who comfort us in all our sorrows, so that we can offer others, in their sorrows, the consolation that we have received from God ourselves. Indeed, as the sufferings of Christ overflow to us, so, through Christ, does our consolation overflow. When we are made to suffer, it is for your consolation and salvation. When, instead, we are comforted, this should be a consolation to you, supporting you in patiently bearing the same sufferings as we bear. And our hope for you is confident, since we know that, sharing our sufferings, you will also share our consolations.

(2 Cor 1:3-8)

The peace of Christ's resurrection, life in the Spirit, was realised for Paul in overcoming the moment when he nearly despaired.   In chapter 4 we see how Paul as a servant of the Servant lived out his mission:

We are only the earthenware jars that hold this treasure, to make it clear that such an overwhelming power comes from God and not from us. We are in difficulties on all sides, but never cornered; we see no answer to our problems, but never despair; we have been persecuted, but never deserted; knocked down, but still have some life in us: always we carry around in us the death of Jesus, so that the life of Jesus, too, may always be seen in our body. Indeed, while we are still alive, we are consigned to our death every day, for the sake of Jesus, so that in our mortal flesh the life of Jesus, too, may be openly shown. So death is at work in us, but life in you.

But as we have the same spirit of faith that is mentioned in scripture – I believed, and therefore I spoke – we too believe and therefore we too speak, knowing that he who raised the Lord Jesus to life will raise us with Jesus in our turn, and put us by his side and you with us. You see, all this is for your benefit, so that the more grace is multiplied among people, the more thanksgiving there will be, to the glory of God.

(2 Cor 4: 7-15)

There is still another limitation for the Servant of the Servant, Paul. He has to face his own humanity and weakness. Thérèse of Lisieux had said that true sanctity consists in our bearing patiently with our weaknesses (LT 243). Paul too spoke of his 'thorn in the flesh'.

In Chapter 12 he tells the Corinthians:

In view of the extraordinary nature of these revelations, to stop me from getting too proud I was given a thorn in the flesh, an angel of Satan to beat me and stop me from getting too proud! About this thing, I have pleaded with the Lord three times for it to leave me – but he has said, 'My grace is enough for you: my power is at its best in weakness'. So I shall be very happy to make my weaknesses my special boast so that the power of Christ may stay over me, and that is why I am quite content with my weaknesses, and with insults, hardships, persecutions, and the agonies I go through for Christ's sake. For it is when I am weak that I am strong.

(2 Cor 12: 7-10)

Paul knew what it was to be tempted to self-righteousness. His "thorn in the flesh" which was not removed but taught him that in the end it by God's grace he was called. His "weakness" became his strength in God. He feels the protection of Christ's power over him. "For when I am weak, then I am strong." (2 Cor 12:10).

All of us are fallible with weaknesses. Paul's confession is a great consolation and shows us that the true source of hope lies elsewhere.

(b) Thérèse of Lisieux: The devotion to Thérèse infuriated some theologians like Rahner, but her charm continues to attract people. She discovered her vocation to 'love' in reading Paul's hymn to love in 1Cor13. Mary of Nazareth was the model for putting this love into practice. Mary is the little way.

However in the last eighteen months of her life she embodied this love in the form of being a suffering servant of the Servant. All feelings of love and consolation dried up. Her mental health suffered with her decline in physical health. In her account of this night we read the following in Manuscript C of the *"Story of the Soul":*

Your child, however, O Lord, has understood Your divine light, and she begs pardon for her brothers. She is resigned to eat the bread of sorrow as long as you desire it; she does not wish to rise up from this table filled with bitterness at which poor sinners are eating until the day set by You. Can she not say in her name and in the name of her brothers, "Have pity on us, O Lord, for we are poor sinners!". Oh! Lord, send us away justified.

126

May all those who were not enlightened by the bright flame of faith one day see it shine. O Jesus! If it is needful that the table soiled by them be purified by a soul who loves You, then I desire to eat this bread of trial at this table until it pleases You to bring me into Your bright Kingdom. The only grace I ask of You is that I never offend You!

(The Story of a Soul, p. 212)

And there is a darker passage later:

Then suddenly the fog that surrounds me becomes more dense; it penetrates my soul and envelops it in such a way that it is impossible to discover within it the sweet image of my Fatherland; everything has disappeared! When I want to rest my heart fatigued by the darkness that surrounds it by the memory of the luminous country after which I aspire, my torment redoubles; it seems to be that the darkness, borrowing the voice of sinners, says mockingly to me: "You are dreaming about the light, about a fatherland embalmed in the sweetest perfumes; you are dreaming about the eternal possession of the Creator of all these marvels; you believe that one day you will walk out of this fog that surrounds you! Advance, advance; rejoice in death which will give you not what you hope for but a night still more profound, the night of nothingness."

Dear Mother, the image I wanted to give you of the darkness that obscures my soul is as imperfect as a sketch is to the model; however, I don't want to write any longer about it; I fear I might blaspheme; I fear even that I have already said too much.

(The Story of a Soul, p. 213)

In the First World War the book *'The Story of a Soul'* became a great source of comfort to those who faced the horror of the trenches. She was a sister to the broken. In Ireland too when her relics came many more people came than had been expected, to see her relics. Many saw in her a sister who shared their darkness and sought to bring the light of Jesus there. Georges Bernanos used the figure of Therêse to help form his characters – characters such as Chantal de Clergerie in Joy and the unknown priest in *The Diary of a Country Priest*. In *The Diary*, the priest realises that he is a victim of the divine agony. In his letter to the English Bernanos wrote the following expression: "You are the sacramental species of the Sacrament of God's Permanent Humiliation".

(c) Gerard Manley Hopkins: Hopkins was a lonely man, never quite fitting in and experiencing deep depression and loneliness. From these experiences grew his poetry.

These have become much loved and those who read them often find consolation. One of the 'terrible sonnets', *'Carrion Comfort'*, expresses Hopkins' state as the end of his life approached:

NOT, I'll not, carrion comfort, Despair, not feast on thee;
Not untwist – slack they may be – these last strands of man
In me or, most wary, cry I can no more. I can;
Can something, hope, wish day come, not choose not to be.
But ah, but O thou terrible, why wouldst thou rude on me
Thy wring-world righ foot rock? Lay a lion limb against me:

Scan

With darksome devouring eyes my bruised bones?   And fan,

O turns of tempest, me heaped there; me frantic to avoid thee and flee?

Still his basic vision of Christ, what he called a 'Christed', vision remained. All the time, Hopkins looked to the comfort of the resurrection. In his 1888 poem, "That Nature is a Heraclitean Fine and of the Comfort of the Resurrection', he wrote at the end:

But vastness blurs and times beats lvel.   Enough! The Resurrection,
A heart's-clarion!   Away grief's gasping, joyless days,
Dejection.
Across my foundering deck shone
A beacon, an eternal beam.
Flesh face, and mortal brash
Fall to the residuary worm; world's wildfire, leave but ash;
In a flash, at a trumpet crash,
I am all at once what Christ is, since he was what I am, and
This Jack, joke, poor potsherd, patch, matchwood, Immortal diamond,
Is immortal diamond.

Through his suffering, Hopkins is still called to new life. He saw his poetry as a form of sacrament. Through it the reader could be led from the darkness of despair to the brightness of new life.

In the words of St. Paul death was at work in him but life in the reader. (cf. 2 Cor 4:4).

St. Francis:

Part of the vocation of the prophet was to do prophetic acts. The lives of Jeremiah, Isaiah and Ezekiel all have instances of this. I find St. Francis and his following of Lady Poverty a profound prophetic act. I am well aware of the tenets of people who speak of the 'vulgar displays of wealth' they see in our lives.

A Swiss priest who died in 1975 helped me understand St. Francis better. The priest's name was Maurice Zundel. He said Lady Poverty was another name for God. God, for Zundel, was one who gave himself away.   We see this in the 'kenosis' of Jesus. Total self-giving in love is the very nature of God. (cf. Donze, *La Pensee Theologique de Maurice Zundel,* pp. 133-137). This was why St. Francis fell in love with Lady Poverty. He fell in love with love.

When Maurice was young he had a friend who introduced him to Victor Hugo and his work entitled, '*Les Miserables*'. The escaped convict Jean Valjean stole candlesticks from the bishop, Myriel. Valjean was caught stealing but the bishop gave Valjean the candlestick. This act of generosity inspired the youthful Zundel. Later in life his friend took his life. Zundel spoke rarely of this but he gave of himself to heal the wounds of those who suffered. That was how he embraced Lady Poverty.

Bernanos, too, showed how Francis and his prophetic acts inspired so many. The following two texts are very precious to me:

In reality, the intelligence does not grow indignant over suffering; rather, it rejects suffering just as it rejects a badly constructed syllogism, which nevertheless the intelligence may later on itself use according to its

130

methods once it has corrected the errors in the syllogism. Whoever speaks of Suffering as an intolerable violation of the soul or, simply, as a fundamental absurdity is sure to receive the approval of imbeciles. But, compared to the small number of those who experience a sincere revolt, how many others are there who, in their revolt against suffering, are only looking for a more or less sly justification for their own indifference and selfishness in the face of those who suffer? *If this were not so, then by what miracle does it happen that precisely those who accept the most humbly, and without understanding it, the permanent scandal of suffering and misery are almost always the very same ones who devote themselves the most tenderly to the care of the suffering and the miserable, for instance, St. Francis of Assisi and Saint Vincent de Paul?*

(Liberte, p. 280)

This is in contrast to the revolts of Ivan in the Brothers Kororazov' who rebels against God because of the suffering of innocent children. In contrast Alyosha goes out to try and ease the suffering of the weak and broken especially children. This is the second meditation of Bernanos that interested me:

Whoever pretends to reform the Church with the same means used to reform temporal society; not only will he fail in his undertaking, but he will infallibly end by finding himself outside the Church. I say that he finds himself outside the Church before anyone has gone to the trouble of excluding him from her. I say that it is he himself who excludes himself from her by a kind of tragic fatalism. ... *The only way of reforming the Church is to suffer for her.* The only way of reforming the visible

131

Church is to suffer for the invisible Church. The only way of reforming the vices of the Church is to lavish on her the example of one's own most heroic virtues. It's quite possible that Saint Francis of Assisi was not any less thrown into revolt than Luther by the debauchery and simony of prelates. We can even be sure that his suffering on this account was fiercer, because his nature was very different from that of the monk of Wittenberg. But Francis did not challenge iniquity; he was not tempted to confront it; instead, he threw himself into poverty, immersing himself in it as deeply as possible along with his followers. He found in poverty the very source and wellspring of all absolution and all purity. Instead of attempting to snatch from the Church all her ill-gotten goods, he overwhelmed her with invisible treasures, and under the hand of this beggar the heaps of gold and lust began blossoming like an April hedge. Ah, yes: I'm well aware that in these matters, comparisons aren't worth much, especially when seasoned with a little humour. Would you still allow me to say, however, in order to be better understood by some readers, that what the Church needs is not critics but artists? ... When poetry is in full crisis, the important thing is not to point the finger at bad poets but oneself to write beautiful poems, thus unstopping the sacred springs.

(Esprit, October, 1951, pp. 439-440)

CHAPTER V: Jesus and the Cross

In the literal sense the word 'cross' refers litterally to an ancient instrument of torture used to crucify those sentenced to death, it was a death Jesus was subjected to; it can also refer to crucifixes, decorations etc. In the figurative sense the word 'cross' refers to all that is entailed by the option for Christ or in his service. (Mtt 5:11; Phil 1:29; 2 Thess 1:5, 2Tim 1:8, 2:8 etc.) The meaning has been widened to include all the trials and difficulties met with in life and borne in vain with the suffering Christ.

Very early on the Cross of Christ was regarded as the greatest manifestation of God's love (Rom 5:6ff, Col 3:19ff). According to the holy tradition of the Church the Cross is the crucible in which God fashions the saints. In its many forms it normally accompanies the decision to follow Christ (Mk, 8:34) and to give one's life out of love as he did.

In the second part of the twentieth century Christian spirituality had tended to stress the resurrection. Although the Easter Alleluia is the triumphant cry hailing the victory of life over the death and suffering that took place on Good Friday, suffering and death are also really present. Death and resurrection are mutually inclusive. They are two aspects of the same mystery. The mystery of the cross and resurrection is a mystery of love (GS 52) and of liberation (GS 52:DH11).

Some feel that devotion to the Cross has to be replaced or superceded by a commitment to helping suffering humankind. In many instances psychology and social work replace the cross.. In Mtt. 25: 44-45, Jesus speaks of being

133

hungry, naked and in prison, a stranger etc. In hearing the cry of the distressed we hear Jesus today.

It is sad that some see devotion to the Cross as something turned in on itself and not open to the pain of Jesus today in the world. The contemplation of Christ crucified opens us to the defenceless love of God revealed in Jesus, it opens us to the reality of human distress and in union with the crucified and risen Jesus leads us to work with him in easing human misery and distress. St. Francis' contemplation of the crucified Lord led him to ease the pain and isolation of the lepers.

One of the great thinkers of the New Testament along with John and Paul was the author of the Letter to the Hebrews. In his words the letter was a word of exhortation (13:22) to those who had grown discouraged and confused and needed to be re-focussed and re-directed. He reflected on the person of Jesus and his cross, and how he had now become the new high priest who interceeded for his people.

He begins his word of encouragement or exhortation by a very beautiful opening paragraph, which helps us see how God acts in Jesus:

At various times in the past and in various different ways, God spoke to our ancestors through the prophets; but, in their own time, the last days, he has spoken to us through his Son that he has appointed to inherit everything and through whom he made everything there is. He is the radiant light of God's glory and the perfect copy of his nature, sustaining the universe by his powerful command; and now that he has destroyed the defilement of sin, he has gone to take his place in heaven at the right hand of divine Majesty – So he is now as far above the angels as the title which he has inherited is higher than their own name.

(Heb 1:1-4)

God spoke in ancient times through the prophets. These include not just the writing prophets but also include Abraham (Gen 20:7), Moses (Deut 28:18), Aaron (Ex 7:1) and Elijah (1Kg18:22). There is continuity between Jesus and the prophets. However, the events of Jesus' life, death and resurrection show that there is also a qualitative difference.

Jesus is the 'radiant light of God's glory'. The glory of God is his divine nature as reflected to humankind. (Jn 1:4). In the Old Testament the divine glory comprises the radiance, righteousness and power of God. Jesus is also the perfect copy of God's nature. The author does not reflect metaphysically on how this came to be. He is content to assert the reality of the son's representation. He is the power, the wisdom of God who sustains the universe. Dante in the final cantico in the 'Divine Comedy' describes how he came to peace in the vision of the love that sustains all things in the universe:

Within its depthless clarity of substance
I saw the Great Light shine into three circles
In three clear colours bound in one same space;
The first seemed to reflect the next like rainbow
On rainbow, and the third was like a flame,
Equally breathed forth by the other two.
How my weak words fall short of my conception,
Which is itself so far from what I saw
That "weak" is much too weak a word to use!
O Light Eternal fixed in Self alone,
Known only to Yourself, and knowing Self,
You love and glow, knowing and being known!
That circling which, as I conceived it, shone
In You as Your own first reflect light
When I had looked deep into It a while,

Seemed in itself and in Its own Self-colour
To be depicted with man's very image.
My eyes were totally absorbed in it.
As the geometer who tries so hard
To square the circle, but cannot discover,
Think as he may, the principle involved,
So did I strive with this new mystery:
I yearned to know how could our image fit
Into that circle, how could it conform;
But my own wings could not take me so high –
Then a great flash of understanding struck
My mind, and suddenly its wish was granted.
At this point power failed high fantasy
But, like a wheel in perfect balance turning,
I felt my will and my desire impelled
By the Love that moves the sun and the other stars.

(Par. XXXIII, 118-145)

The love that moves the '... sun and the other stars' is revealed in Jesus.

In chapter 12 we see how this love is expressed. It consists in Jesus facing death but for the sake of the future and the new life in God to which he leads his people.

With so many witnesses in a great cloud on every side of us, we too, then, should throw off everything that hinders us, especially the sin that clings so easily, and keep running steadily in the race we have started. Let us not lose sight of Jesus, who leads us in our faith and brings it to perfection: for the sake of the joy which was still in the future, he endured the cross, disregarding the shamefulness of it, and *from now on has taken his place at the right* of God's throne.   Think of the way he stood such opposition from sinners and then you will not give up for want of courage. In the fight against sin, you have not yet had to keep fighting to the point of death.

(Heb 12: 1-4)

It is only fixing our eyes on Jesus that we can face any crisis of faith or life. Jesus endured the cross in hope and by entering death ended death and with him we can enter into peace with God.

In chapter 2 we have a reflection on the way Jesus leads his people to peace. We read:

As it was his purpose to bring a great many of his sons into glory, it was appropriate that God, for whom everything exists and through whom everything exists, should make perfect, through suffering, the leader who would take them to their salvation. For the one who sanctifies and the ones who are sanctified, are of the same stock; that is why he openly calls them brothers in the text: *I shall annnounce your name to my brothers, praise you in full assembly,* or the text: *In him I hope*; or the text: *Here I am with the children whom God has given me.*

Since all the children share the same blood and flesh, he too shared equally in it, so that by his death he could take away all the power of the devil, who had power over death, and set free all those who had been held in slavery all their lives by the fear of death. For it was not the angels that he took to himself; he took to himself *descent from Abraham.* It was essential that he should in this way become completely like his brothers so that he could be a compassionate and trustworthy high priest of God's religion, able to atone for human sins. That is, because he has himself been through temptation he is able to help others who are tempted.

(Heb 2:10-18)

Jesus is the one shown as sharing the situation and pain of believers and thereby as the one who leads us to salvation. The larger context of 2:10-18 is a meditation on Ps 8, which serves to direct attention to Jesus in his humiliation and exultation. Although for a short while he has been made lower than the angels he is now crowned with glory and splendour because he suffered death, so that by the grace of God he might taste death for everyone (v 9).

The dominant theme of the passage is that of the solidarity of the son with his people. The solidarity is affirmed in the statement that the one who makes people holy and those who are made holy are now of the one family (v. 11) and in the list of citations from the psalms and Isaiah (v. 12-13) the sisters and brothers of the psalmist are the congregation of the faithful with whom Jesus lifts his voice in the praise of God. Within this setting Jesus is presented as the one in whom death has been overcome and who is high priest.

In 5: 7-10 this champion and high priest is one who was human in every way, who knew tears, sadness, disappointment and death but all those tears are poured out to God (the Father) on behalf of us all.

> During his life on earth; he offered up prayer and entreaty, aloud and in silent tears, to the one who had the power to save him out of death, and he submitted so humbly that his prayer was heard. Although he was Son, he learnt to obey through suffering; but having been made perfect, he became for all who obey him the source of eternal salvation and was acclaimed by God with the title of high priest *of the order of Melchizedek*.

His is not a '... high priest who is incapable of our weaknesses but he is one who has been tempted in every way that we are.' (Heb 3:15). The true humanity of Jesus is something that lip-service is only often paid to. In much preaching and writing the fact that he was fully human has been pushed to one side. Indeed, Martin Niemoller went so far as to say that Jesus is human, often we are not. Jesus is with us in our weakness to be with us and lead us to new life in him. The humanity of Jesus comes across for me in the Gospel of Mark and it is to that I now turn.

The Cross in Mark:

The first words in the Gospel are "The beginning of the Good News about Jesus Christ, the Son of God" (1:1). Mark, at first blush the easiest of the synoptics, retreats from the advancing interpreters like a rainbow's end. A simple outline it seems: eight chapters to explain who Jesus is, eight to explain that He is going to die. It has an abrupt beginning and a mysterious end. This abruptness and darkness permeates the whole. Mark is a book of secrets, of veils and of mysteries. Where the good news actually is, is not immediately clear.

We are required to enter the world of the narrative and we need understanding. If we were in any doubt about this Mark tells us in his blunt style that this is what we must do:

> To you has been given the secret of the kingdom of God, but for those outside, everything comes in parables, in order that they may indeed look, but not perceive ....
> They were utterly astounded, for they did not understand about the loaves, but their hearts were hardened.
> Then do you also fail to understand?
> Do you still not perceive or understand? Are you hearts hardened? Do you have eyes, and fail to see? Do you

have ears, and fail to hear? Do you not remember? …
Do you not yet understand?
Let the reader understand.
(4:11f, 6:5f, 7:19, 8:17-24, 13:14)

N.T (Tom) Wright says that Mark's whole telling of the story of Jesus is designed to function as an Apocalypse.[1] The word 'apocalypse' in Greek means *revelation*. The reader is constantly asked by the Gospel as a whole to do what the disciples are invited to do in parable – chapter, that is to come closer and discover the secret behind the strange outer story. Behind the figure of Jesus lies Isaiah's suffering servant and the hidden action of God in the servant. The baptism of Jesus, the transfiguration and the words of Peter, Caiphas and the Centurion are moments when the veil is lifted, the eyes are opened and like Elisha's servant "… the reader sees the horses and the chariots of fire about the prophets". (N.T. Wright, p. 395).

Paul speaks of the cross in somewhat analogous terms. In 1 Corinthians 1, he refers to the cross as folly to the Greeks, and to the Jews an obstacle (1 Cor 1:23) but to him it reveals the wisdom of God. Chloe has brought word to Paul about the factions and divisions that grew in Corinth but Paul tells them "… When I come among you … I chose to know nobody but Jesus Christ and him crucified" (1 Cor 2:1-2). The word of the cross is paradoxically fragile, defenceless and yet, at the same time, rich in possibility. It is like a seed (Jn 12:24) which by dying yields a harvest of new life.

---

[1] N.T. Wright, *The New Testament and the People of God*, (London; SPCK, 1992) pp. 390-398. I am grateful to him for those insights provided there.

The Agony of Jesus in Mark:

The word 'agony' has its roots in the Greek word 'agon'. Agon refers to athletic preparation and that moment of strain and anxiety before a competition begins. It helps us see what Jesus went through – his passion. The narrative of Jesus' agony in Gethsemane in the Gospel of Mark has always played a central part in my own spirituality. The narrative is direct, uncluttered and has a rawness about it. Matthew and Luke based their accounts on Mark's but the rawness of his style grated on them and they toned down his language somewhat. Mark's account reads:

> They came to a small estate called Gethsemane, and Jesus said to his disciples, 'Stay here while I pray'. Then he took Peter and James and John with him. And a sudden fear came over him, and great distress. And he said to them; My soul is sorrowful to the point of death. Wait here, and keep awake.' And going on a little further he threw himself on the ground and prayed that, if it were possible, this hour might pass him by. 'Abba (Father)!' he said 'Everything is possible for you. Take this cup away from me. But let it be as you, not I, would have it.' He came back and found them sleeping, and he said to Peter, 'Simon, are you asleep? Had you not the strength to keep awake one hour? You should be awake, and praying not to be put to the test. The spirit is willing, but the flesh is weak; Again he went away and prayed, saying the same words. And once more he came back and found them sleeping, their eyes were so heavy; and they could find no answer for him. He came back a third time and said to them, 'You can sleep on now and take your rest. It is all over. The hour has come. Now the Son of Man is to be betrayed into the hands of sinners. Get up! Let us go! My betrayer is close at hand already.'

(Mk 14: 32-42)

Jesus' compassion is made visible in Mark by his healing stories. He was moved with compassion by their plight. As the letter to the Hebrews reminded us he was tempted in every way that they were. Another way of saying this is that he knew their pain in himself. Here in Gethsemane we see most clearly how fully human he actually was.

'A sudden fear and great distress ' came upon him. Behind these two expressions lies the Greek words "ekthambeisthai' and 'adomein'.   These words in their original carry the meaning of breakdown, total dislocation, alienation and a crushing anxiety. (V. Taylor, *Mark*, p. 552). Nervous breakdown is the closest modern expression that comes close to describing what Jesus faces at this moment. The early Fathers of the Church, such as St. Athanasius, spoke of what Jesus had not assumed (taken to himself) has not been healed. Here Jesus descended into the hell of depression, anxiety and godforsakenness and in so doing became the wounded healer of those who know that place. C. G. Jung arrived at the same conclusions from a different standpoint. From his work at the Burgholzi mental hospital he said it is the wounded physician who heals.   When the doctor speaks out of the depth of his own experience he can be with the patient. So, empathy and compassion are all involved in this process (cf. Van Der Post, *Jung*, p. 128). Jesus here knows the silence of God and the pain of isolation. When we can enter this moment with him we find the wounded healer there with us. In this encounter there is love and as we are loved we can accept ourselves as we are (including the shadow side, the side we prefer to pretend we don't have, at least to others). As we are healed by this love we can be wounded healers in our time to those who feel they are alone.

Jesus cries out in his agony, "my soul is sorrowful even to the point of death" (14:34). For Jesus and his people an honest expression of emotion before God was a sign of deep faith. We saw this in the Book of Lamentations. It was as we saw the same in the Psalms of Lament. Jesus too echoes the desperation of Elijah (1 Kings 19:18) and the complaint of Jonah (4:9).

The voice of lament can be heard in the psalms:

'To thee, O Lord, I cried;
And to the Lord I made supplication
"What profit is there in my death,
if I go down to the pit?
Will the dust praise thee?
Will it tell of they faithfulness:
O Hear, O Lord, and be gracious to me!
O Lord, be thou my helper!"'   *(Ps. 30: 8-10)*

'Do not thou, O Lord, withhold
Thy mercy from me,
Let thy steadfast love and thy faithfulness
Ever preserve me!
For evils have encompassed me
Without number
My iniquities have overtaken me,
Till I cannot see;
They are more than the hairs of my head
My heart fails me.'   *(Ps 40: 11-13)*

'I say to God, my rock:
"Why has thou forgotten me?
Why go I mourning?
Because of the oppression of the enemy?"
As with a deadly wound in my body,
My adversaries taunt me,

143

While they say to me continually,
"Where is your God?"
Why are you cast down, O my soul,
And why are you so disquieted
Within me?'   *(Ps 42: 9-11)*

'Vindicate me, O God, and
Defend my cause against an ungodly people;
From deceitful and unjust men
Deliver me!
For thou art the God in whom I take refuge;
Why hast thou cast me off?
Why go I mourning
Because of the oppression of my enemy?

Why are you cast down, O my soul,
And why are you so disquieted
Within me?'   *(Ps 43: 1-2,5)*

'My heart is in anguish within me,
The terrors of death have fallen
Upon me.
Fear and trembling come upon me.

And I say, "O that I had wings like
A Dove!
I would fly away and be at rest;
Yet, I would wander afar,
I would lodge in the wilderness,
I would hast to find me a shelter
From the raging wind and tempest."   *(Ps 61: 1-3)*

The snares of death encompassed me;
The pangs of Sheol laid hold on me;

I suffered distress and anguish,
Then I called on the name of the Lord;
"O Lord, I beseech thee, save
my life!"

(Ps 116: 3-4)

As Dermot Cox showed, such complaint was a great sign of faith.

In the psalms of Lament there was the faith that in the face of what appears opposite, the prayer of the psalmist is heard. (D. Cox, *Psalms*, p. 4-9). It was an act of great courage for Jesus to enter that place and know the anguish and distress of profound loneliness. Behind it lies the love that lay in his heart.

Fydor Dostoyesky's monk, 'Zossima' says something very beautiful that helps me appreciate the depth of this love:

'... love in action is a harsh and dreadful thing compared with love in dreams. Love in dreams is greedy for immediate action, rapidly performed and in the sight of all. Men will even give their lives if only the ordeal does not last long but is soon over, with all looking on and applauding as though on the stage. But active love is labour and fortitude, and for some people too, perhaps a complete science. But I predict that just when you see with horror that in spite of all your efforts you are getting further from your goal, instead of nearer to it – at that very moment I predict that you will reach it and behold clearly the miraculous power of the Lord who has been all the time loving and mysteriously guiding you.'

(Brothers Karamozov, p. 61)

This is a very profound statement. We all love love, yet active love involves repentence, forgiveness and handing judgement over to God. In Matthew's sermon on the Mount (Chapters 5-7) the model for practical and active love is given.

Reflecting on the harshness and difficulty of love in concrete circumstances is something U2 did and they echoed St Paul in many ways. They wrote a song called *'One'* for their album *'Achthung, Baby'*. It came at a time when friends of theirs found their long-term relationships ending. They saw a time when people they knew were dying of AIDS. U2 themselves were on the verge of breaking up. Bono said in an interview that everywhere he looked at advertisements, television programmes and other media relationships and fidelity were being subverted. He also said that the area of sexuality was handed over to pornographers.

In a world of broken people and much sexual violence I can see what he means. The words of 'One' catch the brokeness of this world. It begins:

One
Is it getting better
Or do you feel the same
Will it make it easier on you
Now you got someone to blame.

Confusion, harsh words and mixed emotions are the product of hurt and betrayal. This comes through strongly in the next part:

Did I ask too much
More than a lot
You gave me nothing

Now it's all I got
We're one
But we're not the same
We hurt each other
Then we do it again.

You say
Love is a temple
Love a higher law
Love is a temple
Love the higher law
You ask me to enter
But then you make me crawl
And I can't be holding on
To what you got
When all you got is hurt.

The reality means there is risk and often failure and hurt.
This is the meaning of Dostoyevsky's statement that love
in reality is a harsh thing.   Jesus brought love to those who
were broken but it led to Gethsemane, loneliness and death.

This is not the only theme of 'One'. The following refrain
runs through the song:

One love
One blood
One life
You got to do what you should

One life
With each others
Sisters
Brothers

One me
But we're not the same
We got to carry each other
Carry each other

One

One

This echoes St Paul's letter to the Corinthians where he tells us:

> Just as a human body, though it is made of many parts, is a single unit because all these parts, though many, make one body, so it is with Christ. In the one Spirit we were all baptised, Jews as well as Greeks, slaves as well as citizens, and one Spirit was given to us all to drink.
> .... but that each part may be equally concerned for all the others. If one part is hurt, all parts are hurt with it. If one part is given special honour, all parts enjoy it.
> *(1 Cor 12:1-2, 25-26)*

All of us are responsible for each other – it is in this real situation of human weakness, failure and brokenness that we are called in Jesus to express love. It is in the same context that Paul develops his theology of the variety of gifts given to each. The gift given to each one is meant for the good of all. When I reflect on this passage I see my own weaknesses and failures. It is the type of brokenness that U2 have the courage to articulate. The giftedness of each individual and the contribution each could make to holding up the other was appreciated by St. Francis. In the *'Mirror of Perfection'* (n. 85) he spoke of the perfect friar as one who had the perfect faith and love of poverty of Brother Bernard, the simplicity and purity of Brother Leo and the courtesy of Brother Angelo. Each had a gift for the good of all. The harsh words of "One" remind me that there is often failure to live up to the dignity of who we are in God. That is why Jesus entered the night of pain and doubt to heal us and lead us to life in Him. One of the great tragedies of Christian life is how seldom we turn to the source of all love and deny ourselves the love we need. "Grace brings beauty out of ugly things" and "for those who love God everything acts together into good" (Rom 8-28).

Around Jesus are three disciples: Peter, John and James. Of the group Jesus chose these three seem to constitute an inner good. They were witnesses to the event of the transfiguration in Chapter 9. Here Jesus asks them to be with him. In an incredible act of insensitivity they sleep. The entire career of the disciples is punctuated by this insensitivity. After the miracle of the loaves (8: 1-10), Jesus and the disciples leave the area on a boat. Jesus sets about to instruct the disciples. When he gives them a warning about the yeast of the pharisees, the disciples interpreted this to mean that Jesus is angry because they did not have enough food. The exasperation in Jesus is palpable. This is Mark's account:

> The disciples had forgotten to take any food and they had only one loaf with them in the boat. Then he gave them this warning. 'Keep you eyes open; be on your guard against the yeast of the Pharisees and the yeast of Herod'. And they said to one another, 'It is because we have no bread'. And Jesus knew it, and he said to them, 'Why are you talking about having no bread? Do you not yet understand? Have you no perception? Are

your minds closed? Have you *eyes that do not see, ears that do not hear?* Or do you not remember? When I broke the five loaves among the five thousand, how many baskets full of scraps did you collect? They answered, 'Twelve'. And when I broke the seven loaves for the four thousand, how many baskets of scraps did you collect? And they answered, 'Seven'. Then he said to them, 'Are you still without perception?'

(Mk 8: 14-20)

In chapter 9:30-32 Jesus warns the disciples that he is to suffer and die, but they do not listen because they are arguing about which one is the greatest. Jesus calls a little child to him and tells them "... anyone who welcomes one of all these little ones in my name welcomes me and anyone who welcomes me welcomes not me but the one who sent me." (9:37). In chapter 10: 32-34, we have the second prediction of the passion but this is followed by the request of James and John that they be given the highest place in Jesus' Kingdom. Jesus speaks to them of the cup he must drink, that is the cup of suffering he mentions in Gethsemane. As for the seats on his right and left, they belong to others. This is an oblique reference to the cross – two thieves will occupy those places (10: 35-40).   The will to power and selfish misery can blind us to the needs of those about us. Yet these fallible men are the ones Jesus loved and called. It is for love of such as these that Jesus consented to the cross in Gethsemane when he said: "Not my will but thine" (14:36). It was for the self-righteous pharisees who were blind to their own weaknesses that Jesus reserved his harsh words. The Russian mystics have a saying that the one who knows his own sin is greater than the one who can raise the dead.   Then we know our need of God and we see in Jesus' self-giving the revelation of that love. Jurgen

Moltmann says that Jesus is never more divine than in his self-giving in love expressed on the cross. (Moltmann, *Crucified God,* p. 204).

The account of Jesus' death is stark in Mark's hands. Jesus cries out: 'My God, my God, why have you forsaken me?' It is the voice of Ps 22. It is at once a call to God who is absent and still includes a faith that God still hears even in his silence (cf Chapter 3). Jesus dies with a loud scream!

This is Mark's account:

The death of Jesus:

When the sixth hour came there was darkness over the whole land until the ninth hour. And at the ninth hour Jesus cried out in a loud voice, 'Eloi, Eloi, lama sabachthani?; which means, 'My God, my God, why have you deserted me?' When some of those who stood by heard this, they said, 'Listen, he is calling on Elijah'. Someone ran and soaked a sponge in vinegar and, putting it on a reed, gave it him to drink saying, 'Wait and see if Elijah will come to take him down.' But Jesus gave a loud cry and breathed his last. And the veil of the Temple was torn in two from top to bottom. The centurion, who was standing in front of him, had seen how he had died, and he said, 'In truth this man was a son of God.'

(Mk 15: 32-39)

It is a lonely and sad account, yet at the end the centurion, the foreigner, detects that behind all the events he has witnessed God somehow works. Jesus has lived the Suffering Servant vocation in a new and radical way. The centurion points out to the fact that the last scream of Jesus is not the end.

Blaise Pascal said in his *Pensées* that Jesus' agony continues until the end of life. Caryll Houselander, who was estranged from the church for a time, had a series of what she called her "visions". She had a vision of the Tsar of Russia and Jesus' face becoming one. A while later she was on the tube in London and all of a sudden she perceived in all the face of Christ. Their suffering was his (Houselander, *Born Catholics*, p. 254, 259). Catherine De Hueck Doherty, a Russian émigré, too had an important insight. One day she saw a film about the Tsar and Tsarina and all of a sudden she was crushed by a sense of loneliness. She retired to her Poustinia and prayed and realised that this loneliness was her special vocation. It gave her an insight into the loneliness of God who was once driven out and crucified and it helped her see the loneliness of the world and its people without God. She saw her life as a journey to the lonely Christ in his people and her vocation was to ease the pain of the lonely Christ in all his brothers and sisters (De Hueck Doherty, *Poustinia*, p. 202ff)

Jurgen Moltmann says of the healing power of the cross:

'... It can be summed up by saying that suffering is overcome by suffering, and wounds are healed by wounds. For the suffering in suffering is the lack of love, and the wounds in wounds are the abandonment, and the powerlessness in pain is unbelief. And therefore, the suffering of abandonment is overcome by the suffering of love, which is not afraid of what is sick and ugly, but accepts it and takes it to itself in order to heal it.'

(Crucified God, p. 46)

Marks' account of the resurrection turns the reader off the book. It too is full of anxiety and veiled secrets. In the first four centuries manuscript evidence shows that what we call Mk 16:1-8 is actually the end of the Gospel. Two other endings were added later and they are now joined together in what we call Mk 16: 8-20.

Mk 16: 1-8 is full of allusions to new life. The day is bright compared to the darkness of Calvary. The women are greeted by a young man who stands in stark contrast to the young man who ran away naked at Jesus' arrest (14:51). Jesus is risen, death has been defeated and there is a hint of new life bursting out all over.

When the Sabbath was over, Mary of Magdala, Mary the mother of James and Salome, bought spices with which to go and anoint him. And very early in the morning on the first day of the week they went to the tomb, just as the sun was rising.

They had been saying to one another, 'Who will roll away the stones for us from the entrance to the tomb?' But when they looked they could see that the stone – which was very big – had already been rolled back. On entering the tomb they saw a young man in a white robe seated on the right-hand side, and they were struck with amazement. But he said to them, 'There is no need for alarm. You are looking for Jesus of Nazareth, who was crucified: he has risen, he is not here. See, here is the place where they laid him. But you must go and tell his disciples and Peter, "He is going before you to Galilee; it is there you will see him, just as he told you." And the women came out and ran away from the tomb because they were frightened out of their wits; and they said nothing to a soul, for they were afraid. ..

(Mk 16: 1-8)

The angel tells the women that Jesus is risen and that they are to go and tell the disciples that he is gone before them to Galilee. Nothing is there to prepare us for the shock ending. The women ran away, frightened out of their wits, saying nothing to anyone. Mark's account ends with the Greek word "gar" (16:8). This too was a shock for readers of Greek – nobody did that! Mark in his storytelling does not give us any reason for this shock ending. Once again, the reader is pushed to enter the world of the text and see where can they find meaning.

The Danish philosopher, Kierkegaard, spoke of the concept of 'anxiety'. This anxiety or dread comes to us when we face a new world, new horizons and leave old ways behind. The totally new event of Jesus' triumph over death had this effect for the women and for us who read the text. The old ways are now gone. Dread and anxiety is the initial reaction before we embrace the new ways fully. We have to live under the sign of the Cross, as Mark's readers who suffered persecution, had to. We have to push forward to a future hope as yet unseen.

Living Under the Sign of the Cross:
Good Friday and Easter Saturday people

Living under the sign of the cross means facing a world that is often cruel. In one of the icons of the Easter it shows the risen Christ with the cross in his hands. The end of the cross is plunged into the darkness, the darkness is being overcome but we must wait for the fullness of time before the darkness is overcome. In Hebrews 11:1 we read: "Now Faith is the assurance of things hoped for, the conviction of things not seen." (Heb 11:1).

Albert Camus was always upset by the agony of innocent suffering. He once said, "I am not an atheist nor am I a believer." He was a seeker of truth. In his work, *'La Peste'*, (*The Plague*) he shows the priest Paneloux and Doctor Rieux stand by helplessly as a child dies in agony:

In the presence of the dead child Paneloux says: "Perhaps we should love what we cannot understand. But Dr Rieux answers: "No, Father, I've a very different idea of love. And until my dying day I shall refuse to love a scheme of things in which children are put to torture. And again: "What I hate is death and disease, as you well know."

Péguy's play *Jeanne d'Arc* (1897) is dedicated "to all the men and women who will die their human death for trying to remedy the universal human evil." Saddened and bewildered, the shepherdess of Domremy ponders the existence of universal evil. She is haunted, obsessed, by the wretchedness of the wounded, the sick, the abandoned, the starving, sinners and the damned. "Why does the good Lord allow so much suffering?" She feels helpless before the inexorably rising tide of viscid evil, sin and sacrileges of every kind. She can no longer pray.

Her own soul is crushed as she sees other souls being eternally lost. She goes so far as to offer herself without limit for human suffering in order to save the damned from eternal suffering:

And if to save from eternal Absence
The damned souls infatuated with this Absence
I must long subject my own soul to human suffering,
Then let me live on in human suffering.

With great difficulty Joan of Arc submits to God who has undoubtedly acted for the best. She is unable, however, to be merely resigned: no, we must act, we must resist evil.

Dostoyevsky, for his part, is obsessed by the problem of freedom, rebellion, evil, and the suffering of the innocent; this problem is the central focus of *The Brothers Karamazov*. Ivan Karamazov's speech against God and the absurdity of creation is so radical, so strong, and so searching that Dostoyevsky himself was frightened and had to ask himself whether he would be able to come up with an adequate answer.

"Nowhere in Europe," he said, "is so powerful a defense of atheism to be found. My own belief in Christ and confession of him are thus not those of a simple child. My Hosannah has emerged from a crucible of doubt." Dostoyevsky's answer would, in fact, not take the form of a point by point refutation of the arguments offered by atheism. He would present his readers not with a reasoning process but with a human being; his answer is the monk Zossima – his life, his person, his practice, and his love. For Dostoyevsky, as for us here, there is no argument that can be used as a club to beat back the vast bulk of evil. God's answer is not a discourse, but an action, a passion, a love-filled silence. God answers by allowing his innocent Son to die on the cross. There is something more extravagant, something mightier than the power of evil: the seductive power of defenseless love.

The response to the problem of evil is not refutation, but a figure, a person, a face tormented by suffering that is accepted with love.[2]

Maurice Zundel, too, used to get angry at the expression that God allows suffering. He said look at God's son, he is

---

[2] See R. Latourelle, *Man and His Problems*, (New york: Alba House, 1985) p. 279

the first victim, but by his death gives us hope for new life with him as he rose from the dead.

Dietrich Bonhoeffer was another man who lived under the sign of the Cross. He became a theologian and he confessed later that he had a conversion experience and became a man of prayer. In the face of the rise of Hitler he initially hoped to organise nonviolent protests Gandhi-style against its excesses. He had hoped to go to India to learn from Gandhi that art of peaceful resistance but events overtook him as Europe was plunged into war. He got involved in a plot to kill Hitler but he was caught and executed at Flossenburg. He had told his students to read George Bernanos's book entitled *'The Diary of a Country Priest'*. The priest described his vocation as being one with Jesus in his agony in Gethsemane. The cure says:

The truth is that I've always been in the Garden of Olives. And at the moment – yes, it's strange – at the very moment when he puts his hand on Peter's shoulder and asks the question – the very useless and almost naïve but oh so courteous and tender question – *Are you sleeping?* ... I opened my mouth and was going to answer, but I couldn't. Too bad! Is it not enough that today, through the mouth of my old friend and counsellor, our Lord has done me the grace of revealing to me that nothing would ever snatch me from the place chosen for me from all eternity, my position as prisoner of *the Holy Agony?*

This was doing theology under the sign of the Cross said Bonhoeffer.

W. H. Auden wrote a poem about Bonhoeffer entitled: 'Friday's Child':

Friday's Child
(In memory of Dietrich Bonhoeffer,
Martyred at Flossenburg, April, 9th. 1945)

W. H. Auden

He told us we were free to choose
But, children as we were, we thought –
'Paternal Love will only use
Force in the last resort

On those too bumptious to repent' –
Accustomed to religious dread,
It never crossed our minds he meant
Exactly what He said.

Perhaps he frowns, perhaps He grieves,
But it seems idle to discuss
If anger or compassion leaves
The bigger bangs to us.

What reverence is rightly paid
To a Divinity so odd
He lets the Adam whom He made
Perform the Acts of God?

It might be jolly if we felt
Awe at this Universal man
(When kings were local, people knelt);
Some try to, but who can?

The self-obsessed observing Mind
We meet when we observe at all

Is not alarming or unkind
But utterly banal.

Though instruments at its command
Make wish and counter-wish come true,
It clearly cannot understand
What it can clearly do.

Since the analogies are not
Our sense based belief upon,
We have no means of learning what
Is really going on,

And must put up with having learned
All proofs or disproof that we tender
Of His existence are returned
Unopened to the sender.

Now, did He really break the seal?
And rise again? We dare not say:
But conscious unbelievers feel
Quite sure of Judgement day.

Meanwhile, a silence on the cross,
As dead as we will ever be,
Speaks of some total gain or loss,
And you and I are free

To guess from the insulted face
Just what Appearance He saves
By suffering in a public place
A death reserved for slaves.

The 1950's were a lonely time in the life of Auden. However, reading people like Kierkegaard, Barth and then Bonhoeffer led him to new faith and New Hope. He had to live in the face of the silence of the Cross. In Bonhoeffer's letters from prison he sees the suffering of the world as being the suffering of God.

Our call is to ease the suffering of God in the world. He sees God revealed in Jesus.

In a letter to Eberhard Bethge, 16th July, 1944 he considers the pain of God in these terms:

> Before God and with God we live without God. God lets himself be pushed out of the world on to the cross. He is weak and powerless in the world, and that is precisely the way, the only way, in which he is with us and helps us. Matt. 8.17 makes it quite clear that Christ helps us, not by virtue of his omnipotence, but by virtue of his weakness and suffering.
>
> Here is the decisive difference between Christianity and all religions. Man's religiosity makes him look in his distress to the power of God in the world. God is the *deus ex machina*. The Bible directs man to God's powerlessness and suffering; only the suffering God can help.

And in a later letter of the 21st July, to the same man he says:

> I discovered later, and I'm still discovering right up to this moment, that it is only by living completely in this world that one learns to have faith. One must completely abandon any attempt to make something of oneself, whether it be a saint, or a converted sinner, or a

churchman (a so-called priestly type!), a righteous man or an unrighteous one, a sick man or a healthy one. That is what I call this – worldliness; living unreservedly in life's duties, problems, successes and failures, experiences and perplexities. In so doing we throw ourselves completely into the arms of God, taking seriously not our own sufferings, but those of God in the world – watching with Christ in Gethsemane. That, I think, is faith; that is *metanoia*; and that is how one becomes human and a Christian (Cf. Jer. 45). How can success make us arrogant, or failure lead us astray, when we share in God's sufferings through a life in this world?

Only the suffering God can help us to overcome evil and hope guides us to new life in the future.

U2 give voice to the suffering world. In their earlier album, 'The Unforgettable Fire' (1984) we saw something of the new direction the band were taking. They had seen an art exhibition in Hiroshima entitled: *'The Unforgettable Fire'* where the people tried to give vent to their deep sorrow after the explosion of the atomic bomb on their people. Music, art, film, poetry and theatre are painful vehicles for expressing hurt emotions and help us come to terms with them. In our tradition in Ireland our sad songs helped us cope with the tragedy of the famine and the harshness of poor times. The psalms and much of the scriptures came from the same source as all art. They were a cry of the human heart, giving vent to feelings but in the context of faith. 'Wake Up – Dead Man' is one of U2's most powerful songs. The whole album 'Pop' conveys the mood of a world devoid of sense or value, teetering on the brink of collapse.

Wake Up is a song calling to Jesus who seems silent, silent as the tomb. It is a powerful Holy Saturday lament.

They sing out:

> Jesus, Jesus help me
> I'm alone in this world
> And a fucked up world it is too
> Tell me. Tell me the story
> The one about eternity
> WAKE UP WAKE UP DEAD MAN
> WAKE UP WAKE UP DEAD MAN
>
> Jesus, I'm waiting here boss
> I know you're looking out for us
> But maybe your hands aren't free
> Your Father, He made the world in seven
> He's in charge of heaven
> Will you put a word in for me
> WAKE UP WAKE UP DEAD MAN
> WAKE UP WAKE UP DEAD MAN
>
> Listen to your words they'll tell you what to do
> Listen over the rhythm that's confusing you
> Listen to the reed in the saxophone
> Listen over the hum of the radio
> Listen over sounds of blades in rotation
> Listen through the traffic and circulation
> List as hope and peace try to rhyme
> Listen over marching bands playing out their time
> WAKE UP WAKE UP DEAD MAN
> WAKE UP WAKE UP DEAD MAN

There are times when we have to stay beneath the silence
of the Cross.

The Road to Emmaus:

The Gospels of Matthew and Luke were written after Mark. Unlike Mark they contain resurrection appearances. Obviously Mark's shock ending didn't meet all the needs of the churches. It is extremely difficult to talk of what the resurrection is. Many people imagine that the resurrection was just the resuscitation of a corpse. The resurrection was where Jesus passed over from death to life in God. He was not bound by earthly things. He could walk through doors and ultimately go from sight. The incident narrated by Luke is one of my favourite resurrection stories.

The Road to Emmaus

That very same day, two of them were on their way to a village called Emmaus, seven miles from Jerusalem, and they were talking together about all that had happened. Now as they talked this over, Jesus himself came up and walked by their side; but something prevented them from recognising him. He said to them, 'What matter are you discussing as you walk along?' They stopped short, their faces downcast.

Then one of them, called Cleopas, answered him, 'You must be the only person staying in Jerusalem who does not know the things that have been happening there these last few days.' 'What things?' he asked. 'All about Jesus of Nazareth', they answered, 'who proved he was a great prophet by the things he said and did in the sight of God and of the whole people; and how our chief priests and our leaders handed him over to be sentenced to death, and had him crucified. Our own hope had been that he would be the one to set Israel free. And this is

163

not all: two whole days have gone by since it all happened; and some women from our group have astounded us: they went to the tomb in the early morning, and when they did not find the body, they came back to tell us they had seen a vision of angels who declared he was alive.

Some of our friends went to the tomb and found everything exactly as the women had reported, but of him they saw nothing.

Then he said to them: 'You foolish men! So slow to believe the full message of the prophets. Was it not ordained that the Christ should suffer and die and enter into his glory?' Then, starting with Moses and going through all the prophets, he explained to them the passages throughout the scriptures that were about himself.

When they drew near to the village to which they were going, he made as if to go on; but they pressed him to stay with them. 'It is nearly evening' they said, 'and the day is almost over.' So he went in to stay with them. Now while he was with them at table, he took the bread and said the blessing; then he broke it and handed it to them. And their eyes were opened and they recognised him; but he had vanished from sight. They then said to each other, 'Did not our hearts burn within us as he talked to us on the road and explained the scriptures to us?'

They set out that instant and returned to Jerusalem. There they found the Eleven assembled together with their companions, who said to them: 'Yes, it is true. The Lord has risen and has appeared to Simon. They then told their story of what had happened on the road and how they had recognised him at the breaking of bread.

(Lk 24: 13-26)

164

The scene is set where the two are leaving Jerusalem. Jerusalem is an important interpretative key for Luke's gospel. It was the place where Jesus went to complete his mission. The two on the road are leaving Jerusalem because now there is no hope. Then suddenly Jesus comes among them. As they walk along the road he explains the scriptures to them. They ask him to stay with them and they recognise Him in the breaking of the bread. Explaining the word and the breaking of bread refer to the Eucharist. The Eucharist is when the life-giving events of Jesus' passion, death and resurrection are made re-present. The whole incident is a learning curve for the two on the road and for us that the risen Christ is with us. We can read his word, receive at the table of the Eucharist and know that Jesus is with us today.

Charles Péguy wrote about hope which he called the forgotten virtue, yet he sustains faith and love. For a while Péguy left the church. He was appalled at the lack of interest in care for the proleteriat. He was also upset at the idea of Hell and how Christians did not seem to mind consigning those they disagreed with to Hell. He hoped to alleviate suffering whenever he found it and for a time he embraced socialism. He returned gradually to the faith but his wife and children refused to be baptised.

He was at the fringes of the church because of what he thought of as an irregular vision, but he never ceased to hope. His life's work was to fight injustice wherever he found it (most notably in the Dreyfuss affair). He died on the front at the beginning of World War 1.

Péguy sees the saints as the witnesses to God's grace and the bearers of hope to a world that seems dark and cold. In a memorable piece he speaks of God's hope and faith in those he has called:

You must have confidence in God, he certainly had
Confidence in us.
You must trust in God, he has certainly put his trust
In us.
You must hope in God, he has certainly hoped in us.
You must give God a chance, he has certainly given
us a
Chance.
What chance?
Every chance.
You must have faith in God, he has certainly had faith
In us.

(The Portal of the Mystery of Hope, p. 69)

The Cross in Franciscanism:

Bonaventure's image of God is that of condescending love.
Condescending is the sense of moving out to the beloved.
In the 'Mystical Vine' he writes: 'The Just one fell in love
with the iniquitous, the Beautiful one with the ugly, the only
good and the Holy with the sinful and unholy. Oh,
tremendous condecension! See how much he loves us. Who
could explain it well enough? For Bonaventure the term
'condescension' connotes God's overflowing love and
willingness, as Creator and sustainer of the universe, to
enter that creation and reveal through his Son his love for
all. This love is revealed in Jesus' self-giving on the Cross.

Inspired by Francis' stigmata, Clare of Assisi understood
mystical prayer as being united to, and transformed into,
Christ crucified. For Clare, the crucified Christ, the mirror
of the invisible God, becomes the source of her spirituality.
Christ became the core of her spiritual understanding of
love in gazing on the visual image of the crucified One

(Ingrid Peterson, *Clare of Assisi*, 1993). For more than forty years Clare meditated on the cross which, according to legend, told St. Francis to 'go and repair my house' (2 Cel 5). For Bonaventure as well, it is God's nature to be self-communicating love. In Jesus he is revealed not only as a mystery of love, but as a mystery of humble love.

God takes the human community so seriously that he even assumes the pain and death of our existence.

Bonaventure was inspired by the figure of Francis. He was his teacher of the divine mysteries. He allies learning and theology but at the service of prayer and coming to know Jesus crucified and risen.

Much of his material is inspired by Old Testament texts from the Psalms and Isaiah that were applied to Christ (Ps. 22:18): "They have numbered all my bones"; Isa 1:6: Christ suffers from the sole of his foot to the top of his head; Isa 53:4: Christ covered with bruises and wounds like a leper; Ps 45: 2-3: Christ's suffering and beauty is above that of humans; Isa 63:1-2: describes the red apparel of a man in the winepress in *The Tree of Life,* Bonaventure begins with a pericape from Paul's letter to the Galatians, "With Christ I am nailed to the cross" (Gal 2:20) and employs the metaphor of a tree to map the events of Christ's life, dividing the meditation into twelve fruits arranged in three groups, covering the origin, passion, and glory of Christ. In *The Mystical Vine,* Bonaventure builds on the words, "I am the true vine": from John's Gospel (15:1). The events of the Passion are compared to the cultivation, pruning, and tying up of the vine.

Throughout, "Bonaventure stresses the desirability of conforming to the Passion of Christ, participating in his sufferings so that we may regain the image of his divinity." We are invited to embrace the disfigured body of Christ" in language which is physical, intense, and reciprocal. He writes in *The Mystical Vine:* "Let us embrace our wounded Christ whose hands and feet and side and heart were pierced by the wicked vine-tenders. Let us pray that he may deign to tie our hearts, now so wild and impenitent, with the bond of love, and wound them with love's spear (VM 3.6)"

Bonaventure's spirituality is an extensive, more systematic presentation of the spirituality of Francis, one characterised primarily as imitatio Christi. Bonaventure writes of Francis in the *Life:* "A gentle feeling of compassion transformed him into the one who wanted to be crucified." (LM 8.1). This spirituality of the cross, inspired by Francis, is most visible in *The Life of St. Francis,* in which Bonaventure traces the steps of Francis; in *The Tree of Life,* which leads the reader through a series of meditations on the origin, death, and resurrection of Christ so that one might imitate more closely the dynamics of the life of Christ; in several sermons; and in *The Soul's Journey into God,* in which Francis' experience of the cross on Mount Alverna provides the starting point. This keynote theme finds its fulfillment in the final moments of the text, thus making the cross an overarching image for the entire work.

Whoever loves this death can see God... Let us, then, die and enter into darkness. Let us silence all our cares, our desires, our imaginings. With Christ crucified let us pass out of this world to the Father so that when the Father is shown to us, we may say with Philip: *It is enough for us.* Let us hear with Paul: *My grace is sufficient for you,* and rejoice with David, saying: *My flesh and my heart have fainted away: You are the God of my heart, and the God that is my portion forever. (Itin., 7.6)*

Here, "the spiritual journey as enacted by Christ, and by Francis in imitation of Christ, is unthinkable without the mystery of cruciform love." The cross is a presupposition of mystical union. The discussion of the life of Christ, for Bonaventure, revolves around the specifically Franciscan understanding of the poor Christ.[3]

For Bonaventure, Jesus' life had "normative significance in the spiritual search for an authentic human existence. Spirituality is, above all, the journey of the human soul 'into God'. And that journey is made by conforming one's personal life to the mystery of the eternal Word enfleshed in the history of Jesus. The culmination of that life is the cross – the ultimate sign of God' love for humanity. Imitation of the cross has taken endless forms across the centuries. Some of those forms are better left behind, such as the extreme forms of asceticism that characterised some medieval practices. But one effect of meditation on the cross that seems fairly constant across the centuries is its ability to nurture compassion in the viewer. Of course, this presumes that the motivation for contemplation of the cross is love, but when that is the case, it can create an identification with, and sensitivity to, the suffering of others. Leonardo Boff reminds us that compassion is not to be confused with masochism, in which a person stops with the feeling of pain. Rather, compassion means the desire to identify with the pain of another, to feel together with, to suffer in communion. (L. Boff, *Saint Francis*, pp. 27-28).

Francis' devotion to the crucified and the stigmata, the marks of the crucified, which showed in his flesh, also touched the Carmelite, John of the Cross. He wrote of this in his work entitled, *'The Living Flame of Love'*. The 'Living Flame' is God's spirit who pours out his love into our hearts. John's treatment of the "wound of love" in the

---

[3] See Elizabeth A. Dreyer, Mysticism Tangible Through Metaphor in *'The Cross in Christian Tradition'*, ed. Elizabeth A. Dreyer, (New York: Paulist Press, 2000) pp. 24-236

second stanza of 'The Living Flame of Love' distinguishes between a purely internal cauterisation of the soul effected by the Holy Spirit and "another and most sublime way" of burning in which the soul is wounded internally in such a manner that the flame of divine love fills it entirely so that "it seems to the soul that the whole universe is a sea of love in which it is swallowed."

In this latter case God may allow the effect of this interior love to pass outward to the senses "... as was the case when the seraph wounded St. Francis when the soul is wounded by love with five wounds, the effects extend to the body and the wounds are marked on the body, and it is wounded just as the soul is". For John priority is given to love. John compares the soul to wood being burnt in a living flame. The transformation into flame may be painful for a time but in the end the soul becomes fire, aflame with love. It is in this context that he speaks of the dark nights (cf. *Dark Night of the Soul*, Book 2, chapter X).

The Prayer of St Francis

Most High
glorious God
enlighten the darkness of my heart
and give me
true faith,
certain hope,
And perfect charity,
sense and knowledge.
Lord,
that I may carry out
Your holy and true command.

(Francis of Assisi, p. 40)

CHAPTER VI: Wine into Water:

The Gospel of John is known as the maverick Gospel (Robert Kysar). Clement of Alexandria called it the spiritual Gospel in the second century. It is different from the synoptics. John works on more than one level. The story is at once literal and also symbolic and mystical. The narration is meant to involve the reader and lead to faith in the purposes of God, (the Father) in Jesus. (Jn 20: 30-31). Jesus is described as the word of God made flesh (1:4) and a light that shines in the darkness (1: 5-6). For a while the darkness seemed to overcome the light but in the end the light shone through. The narration of the final overcoming of darkness belongs to the Book of 'Apocalypse' or 'Revelation'.

The darkness is exemplified in the experiences of the heart. There are many instances of trying to overcome the darkness. One is exemplified for me in the life and work of the poet, Francis Thompson.   As a medical student Francis became addicted to a drug called laudanum (alcohol with a tincture of opium). The drug led to his eventual death.   He knew many days of loneliness, despair and destitution. After dropping out of medical school he ended up destitute and ill on the streets of London.   He came near to suicide.   One time near Covent Garden he was going to take a fatal dose of laudanum, but felt as if he was restrained by a mysterious hand from doing so.

Another time when he was very ill from tubercolosis and living on the streets a mysterious woman of the night took him in, gave him lodgings and when he began to recover she went away quietly from his life. He never saw her again.

171

During this time of loneliness he wrote poetry and submitted his work to Wilfred Meynell, editor of the magazine, *'Merry England'*. This led to a lifelong friendship. Meynell tried to help him get over his addiction. He arranged for Thompson to retire to a monastery in Sussex where he could take the open air and the monastic silence and solitude helped restore him to health. The monastery was that of the Canons of Premontre in the village of Storrington.

By May 1889 Thompson saw some light at the end of his agonising addiction withdrawal. One evening as he often did, Thompson paused in a priory owned field. Before his eyes the setting sun transformed the sky into an artist's palette of multicoloured lines. He saw his suffering, his limitation and his life wasted on the streets of London and his crippling addiction to laudanum. Now it was spring and all of nature seemed to be reborn again in the countryside and in the cross before which he prayed. He felt rebirth in his soul. In the beauty of the setting sun he saw of Christ's death and resurrection.

When he prayed before the crucifix in the monastery chapel he had an instant of illumination. He saw in the cross a mystical symbol *par excellence*. He saw in Jesus upon the cross, the light of the world. He wrote:

"Thy straight
Long beam his steady on the Cross. Ah me!
What secret would thy radiant finger show?
Of thy bright mastership is this the key?
Is this the secret, then? And is this the woe."
(Ode to the Setting Sun)

Christ died for us and as Julian of Norwich said he would die over and over again, so endless is the love he has for us. After this time Francis wrote his spiritual autobiography in

172

poetic form, *'The Hound of Heaven'*. The poem begins with his flight from reality, the cross and the God who loved him.

> I fled Him, down the nights and down the days;
> I fled Him, down the arches of the years;
> I fled Him, down the labyrinthine ways
> Of my own mind; and in the mist of tears
> I hid from Him, and under running laughter.
> Up vistaed hopes I sped;
> And shot, precipitated,
> Adown Titanic glooms of chasmed fears,
> From those strong Feet that followed, followed after.
> But with unhurrying chase,
> And unperturbed pace,
> Deliberate speed, majestic instancy,
> They beat – and a Voice beat
> More instant than the Feet –
> "All things betray thee, who betrayest Me."

Ultimately, he knows that even as he flees the inner restlessness will not relent. God seeks him more ardently than he could ever seek God.

> All which they child's mistake
> Fancies as lost, I have stored for thee at hom:
> Rise, clasp My hand, and come!"

> Halts by me that footfall:
> Is my gloom, after all,
> Shade of His hand, outstretched carressingly?
> "Ah, fondest, blindest, weakest,
> I am He whom thou seekest!
> Thou dravest love from thee, who dravest Me."

In the light of the crucified he knows that he is loved in all his misery and is being called to have life and have it to the full. During the rest of his years Francis know much depression and many relapses but the inner light could now never be quenched. His poetry became a light in the darkness of many people's lives.

On November, 13th, 1907, Francis Thompson died after years of struggle, loneliness and constant failure, yet he brought light to many. Finally, he knew no more darkness. He saw all his sorrow being caught up by the cross awaiting healing. Before God's love all is transformed; "Grace brings beauty out of ugly things." He describes his own walk in darkness:

L'Envoi

O thou who dwellest in the day!
Behold, I pace amidst the gloom;
Darkness is ever round my way
With little space for sunbeam-room.

Yet Christian sadness is divine
Even as thy patient sadness was:
The salt tears in our life's dark wine
Fell in it from the saving cross.

Bitter the bread of our repast;
Yet doth a sweet the bitter leaven:
Our sorrow is the shadow cast
Around it by the light of Heaven.
O light in Light, shine down from Heaven!

In Jesus' spirit we are transformed as we stand as broken sinners in the need of healing.

The figure of Mary was very important for Francis as he prayed at the Cross. She was mother of Jesus as he entered his lent agony and she stands with all of Jesus' brothers and sisters in their lonely vigil.

Francis wrote of this in his poem entitled: *'Lines from a Drawing of Our Lady of the Night'*:

This, could I paint my inward sight,
This were Our Lady of the Night:

She bears on her front's lucency
The starlight of her purity;

For as the white rays of that star
The union of all colours are,

She sums all virtues that may be
In her sweet light of purity.

The mantle which she holds on high
Is the great mantle of the sky.

Think, O sick toiler, when the night
Comes on her, sad and infinite,

Think, sometimes, 'tis our own Lady
Spreads her blue mantle over thee,

And folds the earth, a wearied thing,
Beneath its gentle shadowing;

Then rest a little; and in sleep
Forget to week, forget to weep!

In his darkest hours the figure of Mary, Mother of Sorrow, gave him hope.

Francis' journey is something like the prayer-journey I am going to undertake with the Gospel of John. Those who join me can see their own darkness under the shadow of the cross and know the consoling presence of Mary, the icon of the Spirit.

The Prologue: (Jn 1:1-18)

The prologue of John probably had a literary pre-history as a hymn of the early Christian community, but John made the hymn his own, adapted it in places and gives an indication of the themes the Gospel narration will catch. The prologue goes as follows:

> In the beginning was the Word:
> The Word was with God
> And the Word was God.
> He was with God in the beginning,
> Through him all things came to be,
> Not one thing had its being but through him.
> All that came to be had life in him
> And that life was the light of men,
> A light that shines in the dark,
> A light that darkness could not overpower.
> A man came, sent by God,
> His name was John.
> He came as a witness,
> As a witness to speak for the light,
> So that everyone might believe through him.
> He was not the light,
> Only a witness to speak for the light.

The Word was the true light
That enlightens all men;
And he was coming into the world.
He was in the world
That had its being through him,
And the world did not know him.
He came to his own domain
And his own people did not accept him.
Bot to all who did accept him
He gave power to become children of God,
To all who believe in the name of him
Who was born not out of human stock
Or urge of the flesh
Or will of man
But of God himself.
The Word was made flesh,
He lived among us,
And we saw his glory,
The glory that is his as the only Son of the Father,
Full of grace and truth.

John appears as his witness He proclaims:
'This is the one of whom I said:
He who comes after me
Ranks before me
Because he existed before me'.

Indeed, from his fulness we have, all of us, received –
Yes, grace in return for grace,
Since, though the Law was given through Moses,
Grace and truth have come through Jesus Christ.
No one has ever seen God;
It is the only Son, who is nearest to the Father's heart,
Who has made him known.

The first idea I look at is John's use of the term *Word* (gk: *logos*).   Francis J. Moloney in his commentary on the Gospel shows that in his own way John is the most Jewish of the Gospels. The term *logos* has its antecedents in the Old Testament. It also creates a dialogue with Greek culture in which *logos* is to the world as the soul is to the body. Philo of Alexandria in the first century also interpreted the Hebrew Bible in dialogue with Greek philosophy.

The Old Testament speaks of the word of God. The word of God is God's speech to show human beings God's will for their healing and right living but it is not yet personified. In Isaiah we read: "yes, as the rain and the snow came down from the heavens and do not return without watering the earth, making it yield and giving growth to provide seed for the sower and bread for the eating, so the word that goes from my mouth does not return to me empty, without carrying out my will and succeeding in what it was sent to do." (Is 55: 10-11)

If we return to the later part of the Old Testament there is found the personification of wisdom. Around the time of the writing of the Book of Proverbs, there was a crisis in the way the people looked at the world.   Job and Qoheleth challenged the old-accepted norms. Qoheleth sought wisdom from his own experience: "All this I have tested by wisdom: I have said, "I will be wise", but it was far from me. That which is, is for all, and deep, very deep who can find it out?" (7: 23f). Proverbs insists that we can know wisdom. She emerges in personified form so that she can speak to human beings. She was present before all works and was present when the creation brought the world to be.

'Yahweh created me when his purpose first unfolded,
before the oldest of his works.
From everlasting I was firmly set,

From the beginning, before earth came into being.
The deep was not, when I was born,
There were no springs to gush with water.
Before the mountains were settled,
Before the hills, I came to birth;
Before he made the earth, the countryside,
Or the first grains of the world's dust.
When he fixed the heavens firm, I was there,
When he drew a ring on the surface of the deep,
When he assigned the sea its boundaries
-and the waters will not invade the shore –
when he laid down the foundations of the earth,
I was by his side, a master craftsman,
Delighting him day after day,
Ever at play in his presence,
At play everywhere in his world,
Delighting to be with the sons of men.

(Proverbs 8: 22-31)

A good century after Qoheleth and the Book of Proverbs Palestine experienced a relatively peaceful development under the *Ptolemeic* kings reigning in Egypt (after 304 B.C.). However, there were tensions between assimilation to Hellenistic culture and the preservation of the Jewish heritage. It was in this tension that the Jewish scribe BenSira appeared and his book (written between 190 and 175 B.C.) is a unique expression of the tension between the Jewish heritage and the contemporary Hellenistic culture. Sirach 24 makes a statement about the foundation of the world. Wisdom is described as a kind of primal mist (24:3) over the earth and wisdom is identified with the divine Logos, the divine creative word which is operative here. Wisdom also appears as the spirit of God which roamed over the primal water, as in Gen 1:2. Sirach says:

Wisdom speaks her own praises,
In the midst of her people she glories in herself.
She opens her mouth in the assembly of the Most High,
She glories in herself in the presence of the Mighty One;
'I came forth from the mouth of the Most High,
and I covered the earth like mist.
I had my tent in the heights,
And my throne in a pillar of cloud.
Alone I encircled the vault of the sky,
And I walked on the bottom of the deeps,
Over the waves of the sea and over the whole earth,
And over every people and nation I have held sway.
Among all these I searched for rest,
And looked to see in whose territory I might pitch camp.
Then the creator of all things instructed me,
And he who created me fixed a place for my tent.
He said, "Pitch your tent in Jacob,
Make Israel your inheritance."

From eternity, in the beginning, he created me,
And for eternity I shall remain.
I ministered before him in the holy tabernacle,
And thus was I established on Zion.
In the beloved city he has given me rest,
And in Jerusalem I wield my authority.
I have taken root in a privileged people,
In the Lord's property, in his inheritance.
I have grown tall as a cedar on Lebanon,
As a cypress on Mount Hermon;
I have grown tall as a palm in Engedi,
As the rose bushes of Jericho;
As a fine olive in the plain,
As a plane tree I have grown tall.

(Sirach, 24: 1-20)

The Book of Wisdom was written in Greek and is an attempt to instil in the Jewish readers a respect for their heritage. It was written in Alexandria in Egypt in the first century B.C.E. The author is looking for a way to overcome suffering and promises immortality for those who persevere in their faith.

In Chapter 9 he says:

> "God of our ancestors, Lord of mercy,
> who by your word (par ton logos) you have
> made all things,
> and in your wisdom (par ta sophia) have fitted
> man,
> To rule the creatures that have come from you,
> To govern the world in holiness and justice,
> And in honesty of soul to disperse fair judgement
> Grant me Wisdom, consort of your throne
> And do not reject me from the number of your
> Children."
>
> ### *(Wisdom, 9: 1-4)*

In this passage we have the idea of wisdom (gk *Sophia*) and word (gk: *Logos*) placed side by side. The Greek *sophia* is a translation of the Hebrew word *hokmah*. In the prologue of John, he used Logos to embrace all that is said about personified wisdom in the works cited. He also alludes to the hebrew term *dabar* which means *word* and is used in Gen 1-2 to describe how God's creative word brought all things into existence. Also, in the *Targumim,* written about the same time as John the Aramaic word *'memra'* is used. This is Aramaic for *'word'* but means God's presence. John's use of the term *logos* catches all the meanings.

We are told the 'Word was with God, and the Word was God' (Jn1:1). This Word became flesh and lived among us (1:14). The pre –existence of the Word is something that the Church has grappled with since the beginning. The major councils of the church grappled with this in the early centuries. Karl – Joseph Kuschel in his work entitled *'Born Before All Time'* contains a beautiful passage which does not explain the mystery but pushes us in a direction to appreciate the depth of what is being said here.

> If God in Jesus Christ has not just revealed part of himself, but has definitively and unrestrainedly revealed his being, then Jesus Christ – as Spirit and in the Spirit – is also present to all time, contemporaneous with all time, and free of all time.   That is precisely what is being said when we use the term 'pre-existence of Christ'.
>
> ***(Born Before All Time, p. 490)***

God is identified by Jesus as Father. "No One has ever seen God, it is the only Son, who is nearest to the Father's heart who has made him known."

(Jn 1:18)

Jesus says in 14:28:

> "If you loved me,
> You would be happy that I am going to the Father
> For the Father is greater than I."
>
> *(Jn 14:28)*

The Father who is called by Jesus "my God" (20:17). He is the central figure in John's Gospel. Everything turns towards the Father.   Calling God "Father" was something distinctive in Jesus' spirituality. In Mark's account of

182

Gethsemane Jesus calls God "Abba" – a term used to indicate intimacy. In Jn 10:30 Jesus tells us that "I am the Father are one."

Philip the Greek-speaking apostle asks Jesus: "Lord, let us see the Father. That is all we ask for."

"For such a long time I have been with you" Jesus answered. "And you still don't know me Philip? Whoever has seen me, has seen the Father. How then can you say, "Make us see the Father." (14:7-9).

Jesus reveals in his person the Father. His whole purpose is to make the Father known (17, 6-26) and to show the world the love of the Father. Meeting the carpenter from Nazareth we are brought into contact with the unseen God in Heaven.

Jesus embodies unconditional and defenceless love. In being defenceless he is led to crucifixion and death – yet, these are overcome in the resurrection. Jesus came as love, as light but many preferred the darkness to the light and refused to accept him (3:19, cf also 1:11). Jesus' wish was for all people to come to the light. (12: 34-50).

Jesus says: "A man can have no greater love than to lay down his life for his flock:"(15:13) and he tells us "As the Father has loved me so I have loved you." (15:9). God loved us, human people, so much that he sent his Son – not to condemn us, but to liberate us from our sins and give us life (3: 16-17). The Father loved us with an everlasting love before the world began (17:24). Father and Son invite us in the Spirit to share in their love (14; 21, 23). God's salvific action proceeds from love and lead to love. The clearest statement of this is found in 1 John. "We know and believe that God loves us. God is love and whoever is immersed in love is immersed in God: and God is in that person." (1 Jn 4:16). God is the ultimate ruler of our destiny and holds us in his love. "There is no room for fear in love. Perfect love gets rid of fear. For fear is related to punishment and a person who is afraid does not love fully". (1 Jn 4:18)

Péguy in his writings displayed this sensitivity to the tenderness of the heart of God. *Heart* in the Bible denotes what we mean by 'person' or 'centre of a person'. Péguy says that all our hope rests on this tender love of God. "That is what God began with. All feelings, all emotion that are one to God, he has already experienced with regard to us." This is not any predestination election but in creation as a whole. "So it is not the will of your Father in Heaven that one of these little ones should perish. See that you do not despise one of these little ones." And "does not the shepherd leave the ninety-nine in the desert to seek the one that was lost until he finds it? I tell you there is as much joy in Heaven over one sinner who repents as over ninety-nine righteous men, who need no repentence." Péguy marvels over the care and love of God for the individual who seems lost. He says in another place: "For it was dead and has come back to life. It has made God's heart tremble with anguish. It has caused an unfamiliar feeling to well up in the heart of God himself, made his heart new, as it were.

The heart of God made new – I have weighed these words. I know what I am saying: the heart of God eternally new" (cf. Von Balthasar, *Glory of the Lord* 11, p. 497f). We are called to enter with Jesus in the Spirit, to enter the Trinity of love. We feel the love of the eternal Thou of God for the human person. We enter into an I – eternal Thou relationship of love. The end of John of the Cross's Canticle describes the experience of Christ awakening us to love in the centre of our being: the heart. "Thou wakest, O Word, O Spouse, in the centre and depth of my soul, in its love and most intimate substance." Jesus is described in the prologue as the light and life of the world (1: 3-5).

The theme of God as *light* is found in the psalms:

"Yes with you is the fountain of life,
by your light we see the light."

(Ps 36:9)

In Jn 8:12 we read: "I am the light of the world, anyone who follows me will not be walking in the dark, but will have the light of life." However, the Word was true life but when he came to his own people they did not accept him (1: 9-12). The darkness tried to overcome him but in his death and resurrection the darkness could not overpower him (1:4f). This helps us keep Jesus in perspective and forces us to take realistically the "darkness".

At the Last Supper Jesus said: "One of you will betray me". He said this with great sorrow. He stretched out his hand, took a morsel of bread, dipped in the herbal sauce and gave it to Judas – an ordinary gesture of oriental hospitality. For Judas it was an offer of friendship, a challenge to turn back again. But Judas looked at Jesus, took the morsel and hardened his heart. "As soon as he took the morsel of food Satan entered into him." (13:37). Judas left and as he went outside "it was night" (13:30). When Jesus rose the night of terror ended (20:1). His ultimate victory was assured (16:33), but the image of the night, of the world of darkness, still holds its validity for us today. In John's eyes many still "walk in darkness" and as Christians we can only stay in God's love by remaining constantly aware of the threat that the darkness may trap and engulf us too. Jesus has overcome the darkness and calls us into his presence to help us on our journey of overcoming the darkness until the day when all the darkness is finally overcome. We are still on a journey but we are not alone. Jesus tells us to take courage from him because he has overcome the world. (16:33).

Georges Bernanos offers us a story of darkness, a darkness from out of hatred. The incident takes place between the unknown cure and the lady of the manor in *'The Diary of a Country Priest'*. The lady lost her child at an early age and ever since has been filled with hatred and rebellion against God. She has it in for him! The priest timidly ventures to speak to her of resignation. The countess replies: "Don't you think me resigned enough? If I hadn't been resigned!"

Hardly aware of what he is saying, the priest continues: "God is not to be bargained with. We must give ourselves to Him unconditionally. Give Him everything. He will give you back even more." At this the countess cries out in wild rage. "Suppose that in this world or the next, somewhere was a place where God doesn't exist ... I'd take my boy to that place ... and I'd say to God: "Now, stamp us out!"

The priest thinks of the sobs, the grasps of agony, torn from the throat of wretched human beings in the midst of suffering and says:

Madame, if our God were a pagan god or the god of the intellectuals ... He might fly to His remotest heaven and our grief would force Him down to earth again. But you know that our God came to be among us. Shake your fist at Him, spit in His face, scourge Him, and finally crucify Him: what does it matter? My daughter, it's already been done to Him ... Hell is not to love any more.

Then, at the end of her strength, exhausted by a struggle that has gone on for eleven years, the countess surrenders. She flings into the fire her child's lock of blond hair which she had kept with her in a locket as a witness against God. She has just escaped from a terrible loneliness, because she had encountered disfigured Innocence and suddenly her heart broke open. Hope entered in, hastening there from the wide spaces, and invaded her like a great breath of spring. In Christ's gaze she had once again found serenity, peace and boundless joy. The next night, doubtless broken by agony she had lived with for so many years, the countess died as a woman reconciled to Love. Two hearts crushed in the same press, but Love had emerged victorious over hatred.

In a like manner, if we want to understand and not run away, we must trust in the cross, which is madness in the eyes of the world but proves to be wiser than any explanation, stronger than any challenge, mightier than any violence. What the cross teaches us is that the first victim of the freedom God has given us is God Himself. The supreme law governing our world is not a cosmic law but the law of the mysterious dialogue between human freedom, which has been endowed with the capability of saying the final word, and the freedom of God, whose final word is not a word but an act, a *passion* which shows us how far sin can go but, at the same time, how far love can go. Here rebellion is not beaten down from outside but is plunged into the abyss of love. Man meets not resistance but outstretched arms. In order to disarm us when we rebel God offers us a superabundance of love. On the cross that stands at the crossroads of the centuries, torn and bloodied love is the counterweight that tips the scale despite all the weight of our sins and offsets all our acts of hatred. The crucified God introduces into the world a love that is greater than all the hatred there may ever be.

We need, therefore, to review all our ideas about God.

Because he respects our free decisions, God allows himself to be crushed and crucified by sin. When David learned of the death of his son, Absalom, he cried: "Would that I had died instead of you, O Absalom, my son, my son!" (2 Sam 19:1). When God sees his children choosing death by refusing to answer his call, he takes their place; he dies for them, he makes himself their "security". The cross thus takes us into a universe that is located completely outside the realm of justice, a universe of love but a love that is *wholly other* and *mysterious*.

The Cross in John:

John's account of the death of Jesus includes a scene where the soldiers divide Jesus' clothing when they throw dice to see which of the soldiers would divide the seamless robe. In this the words of scripture were fulfilled:

> "They shared my clothing among them.
> They cast lots for my robe.
> This is exactly what the soldiers did."

(Jn 19: 23f)

Once again, we have an allusion to Ps 22:18. John's account of the death of Jesus goes on:

> Near the cross of Jesus stood his mother and his mother's sister, Mary the wife of Clopas, and Mary of Magdala. Seeing his mother and the disciple he loved standing near her, Jesus said to his mother: "Woman, this is your son." Then to the disciple he said, "This is your mother." And from that hour the disciple made a place for her in his home.

188

After this, Jesus knew that everything had now been completed, and to fulfil the scripture perfectly he said: *'I am thirsty'.*

A jar-full of vinegar stood there, so putting a sponge soaked in the vinegar on a hyssop stick he held it up to his mouth. After Jesus had taken the vinegar he said, "it is accomplished"; and bowing his head he gave up his spirit.

(Jn 19: 25-30)

The Mother of Jesus and the beloved disciple stand near Jesus in his last agony (19: 26-27). Although his mother was mentioned with the other women in 19:25 she does not become a protagonist until v. 26 where she is joined to the beloved disciple. We last heard of this other disciple in 18:15-16 where, not having gone away with the rest, he followed Jesus to the court of the high priest and got Peter in. Now after Peter had denied Jesus, this disciple is the only faithful role to follow Jesus to the Cross. John's Gospel in its second reference to him at the crucifixion (19:35) makes him the eyewitness and the tradition bearer who guarantees the authenticity of what is in the Gospel.

Jesus begins to speak upon seeing his mother and the disciple. The mother is the first mentioned of the pair. This suggests she is the primary concern of the episode. Neither are addressed by name. The beloved disciple is not identified. Here we are alerted to John's working at more than one level. The beloved disciple has a representative role here. He stands for all who stood by Jesus and trust in him faithfully. Sandra Schneiders points out in her commentary, *'Written That You May Believe'*, that Mary Magdalene fulfills the role of beloved disciple perfectly (p. 219-33, p 150f). Mary, his mother was last heard of at the marriage

189

feast of Cana (2: 1-12) where her initial concern was to fill the needs of the wedding party by an implied plea for Jesus to act.

A wedding feast in the Palestine of Jesus' time lasted for many days and it was a sign of hospitality and welcome for the host to provide enough wine for the feast. We now look back to the wedding feast.

The Wedding at Cana:

Three days later there was a wedding at Cana in Galilee. The mother of Jesus was there and Jesus and his disciples had also been invited. When they ran out of wine, since the wine provided for the wedding was all finished, the mother of Jesus said to him, 'They have no wine.' Jesus said, "Woman, why turn to me?' My hour has not come yet.' His mother said to the servants, *'Do whatever he tells you.'* There were six stone water jars standing there, meant for the ablutions that are customary among the Jews; each could hold twenty or thirty gallons. Jesus said to the servants, 'Fill the jars with water,' and they filled them to the brim. 'Draw some out now', he told them, 'and take it to the steward.' They did this; the steward tasted the water, and it had turned into wine. Having no idea where it came from – only the servants who had drawn the water knew – the steward called the bridegroom and said, 'People generally serve the best wine first, and keep the cheaper sort till the guests have had plenty to drink; but you have kept the best wine till now.'

This was the first of the signs by Jesus; it was given at Cana in Galilee. He let his glory be seen, and his disciples believed in him. After this he went down to

Capernaum with his mother and the brothers, but they stayed there only a few days.

(Jn 2: 1-11)

(a) John's Birth Scene:
Ivone Gebara and Maria Clara Bingemer in their work *'Mary, Mother of God, Mother of the Poor,* say of this passage: "Mary's faith begets and gives birth to the faith of the new messianic community." (p. 80). Mary knew that, with an intuition of prayer and closeness to God that a crucial moment had arrived, that God was again preparing her to step in to the unknown. Tina Beattie builds on this idea (*Rediscovering Mary*, p. 99f). Just as Mary gave birth to Jesus so now she was being asked to push him into the public domain, into a hostile world, into the darkness. Jesus asked her: "What is this to me and you? My hour has not yet come." (2:4). He was, in effect, signalling to her that from now on everything would be changed. They would enter a new relationship – he as Servant and she as a servant of the servant. Xavier Leon-Dufour suggests in his work entitled: *'Lecture de l'Evangile selon Jean, 1,* (p. 203ff) that the statement: '… My hour has not yet come' is actually a question meaning: "Has my hour come?" All of these readings lead to internal coherence in the text when Mary tells the servants: "Do as he tells you". If Mary were rebuked she would not have shown such faith as she acted against her son. By her telling the servants this she is showing herself to be now a disciple, a servant of the Servant and she turns to the other servants, saying: "Do as he tells you" (2:6). The water became wine.

(b) Woman:
Jesus does not refer to his mother as Mary or mother, but as 'woman'. At any level it is an extraordinary way to

191

address a mother. Some of the Fathers said it was a form of politeness. This makes the address even more extraordinary. The word points beyond itself and opens up different viewpoints, different levels. Already at an early stage of Christian exegesis she who is called 'woman' was compared to Eve, the woman of Gen 2-4. Even as Eve was mother of all the living (Gen 3:20) so does this mother become the mother of the beloved disciple.

The image of the woman in labour adds another strand to the text:

> "When a woman is in labour, she has pain because her hour has come. But when her child is born, she no longer remembers her anguish because of the joy of bringing a human being into the world."
>
> *(Jn. 16:21)*

Mary gives Jesus over to his mission and becomes a servant of the Servant in working with him to give life to his brothers and sisters.

The Johannine image in turn evokes passages in Isaiah which portray exiled Israel in torment and labour, yearning to bring faith new life from its barrenness.

> "Sing, O Barren one, who did not bear: burst into song and shout, you who have not been in labour! For the children of the desolate woman will be more than the children of her that is married, says the Lord"
>
> *(Isaiah 54:1)*

Because she was in labour she gave birth; before her pain came upon her she delivered a son. Who has heard such a thing? Who has seen such a thing? Shall a land be born in one day? Shall a nation be delivered in one moment? Yet as soon as Zion was in labour she delivered

192

her children. Shall I open the womb and not deliver? Says the Lord: Shall I, the one who delivers shut the womb? Says your God.

(Isaiah 66: 7-11)

(c) Hour:

Jesus speaks of the 'hour'. The hour is at the moment of the passion. We are told in 19:27 that from that "hour" the disciple took Mary to his home. Jesus referred to the fact that the hour had come in chapter 12:

"Now the hour has come
for the Son of Man to be glorified.
I tell you, most solemnly,
Unless a wheat grain falls to the ground and dies,
It remains only a single grain
But if it dies
It yields a rich harvest.
Anyone who loves his live lose it.
Anyone who hates his life in this world
Will keep it for eternal life.

If a man serves me he must
Follow me,
Wherever I am, my servant will be there
too."

(Jn 12: 23-26)

The servants of the Servant are called to be where Jesus is. At the Cross the servants are the Mother of Jesus and the beloved disciples. The image of the seed dying runs through Dostoyevsky's *"Brothers Karamazov"*. In a pivotal scene the holy man Zossima dies. All the monastery expect a miracle and signs at the death of a holy man but instead the body stinks. Alyosha who idolised Zossima goes through his own moment of doubt. He has been disturbed by Ivan's rebellion against God and his parable of the Grand Inquisitor. Now the holy one dies with no miracle. In this state of mind he returns to the monastery and hears Fr. Paissy reading John's account of the wedding feast of Cana over the dead Zossima. Alyosha collapses into sleep and in the sleep the elder Zossima comes to him.

'And when they wanted wine, the mother of Jesus said unto him, They have no wine,' Alyosha heard:

'Oh yes, I nearly missed that, and I did not want to miss it. I love that passage: it is Cana of Galilee, it's the first miracle. ... Oh, that miracle, oh, that lovely miracle! It was not grief but men's gladness that Jesus extolled when he worked his first miracle – he helped people to be happy. ... "He who loves men, loves their gladness" – that was what the dead man had kept repeating, that was one of his main ideas. ... Without gladness it is impossible to live, says Mitya. ... Yes, Mitya ... Whatever is true and beautiful is always full of forgiveness – that also he used to say. ...'

'Jesus saith unto her, Woman, what have I to do with thee? Mine hour is not yet come. His mother saith unto the servants, Whatever he saith unto you, do it.'

'Do it. .... The gladness, the gladness of some poor, very poor people ... Yes, poor, of course, if they hadn't enough wine even at a wedding. ... Historians write that the people living by the lake of Gennesaret and in all those places were the poorest that can possibly be imagined. ... And another great heart of the other great being, his Mother, who was there at the time, knew that he had come down only for his great and terrible sacrifice, but that his heart was open also to the simple

and artless joys of ignorant human beings, ignorant but not cunning, who had warmly bidden him to their poor wedding. "Mine hour is not yet come" – he said with a gentle smile. (yes, he certainly smiled gently at her). ... And, surely, it was not to increase the wine at poor weddings that he came down on earth. And yet he went and did as she asked him. ... Oh, he is reading again:'
'Jesus saith unto them, Fill the waterpots with water. And they filled them up to the brim.
'And he saith unto them, Draw out now, and bear unto the governor of the feast. And they bore it.
'When the ruler of the feast had tasted the water that was made wine, and knew not whence it was: (but the servants which drew the water knew) the governor of the feast called the bridegroom.
'And saith unto him: Every man at the beginning doth set forth good wine; and when men have well drunk, then that which is worse: but thou hast kept the good wine until now.'

(Brothers Karamazov, p. 424f)

At this Alyosha recovers his strength. The waters of doubt and fear have given way to faith and new life. The death of Zossima (the 'seed') enables him to go forth and live his vocation. Zossima had told him not to be a monk but to live in the midst of people and given them strength (change their water into wine). Alyosha does this at the end when he gives strength to a group of children at a funeral. The true miracle of Zossima's death would be in the hearts of his disciples.

(d) Wine:
The theme of Christian joy is implied in the miracle itself. The element that was lacking at the feast was wine and

wine symbolises the goods things of life, the enjoyment that God grants as gift. "Eat your food with joy and drink your wine with a happy heart: for God shows his approval in them" (Qoheleth 9:7). "What is life worth to someone who has no wine? Wine was created to make people happy" (Sir 31: 27). God gave human beings wine to gladden their hearts (Ps 104: 15). When Jesus changed water into wine he indicated that he was bringing happiness of a new kind. He was offering the abundant joy of life in God where there was healing, salvation and the fullness of life. He invited the lonely and oppressed of all nations to his messianic banquet of rich food and fine wine. (Isa 25: 6-9).

In the Johanine discourse Jesus repeatedly announces this Joy.

"Dear Father, I want my disciple to experience
the fullness of my joy." *(17:13)*

"Your sorrow will turn into joy." *(16:20)*

"Your hearts will rejoice and no one will be able
to take away your joy." *(16:22)*

"Ask in my name and you will receive what you
ask for. In this way your joy will be complete." *(16:2)*

"I want you to experience my joy and I want your
joy to be complete." *(15:16)*

This joy Jesus gives us to experience is closely linked to the abundance of life he brings and to the peace with which he will fill our hearts.

When Joy Davidman married the Belfast-born author, C.S. Lewis, she was amazed at some of the attitudes she found in Christianity. She was a convert from Judaism. She could not understand how Christians could ask the question 'Did Jesus laugh?' or at the lack of joy some brought to Christianity. She explained to Lewis that the Jewish people, of which Jesus was one, treasured love, laughter and joy. They laughed at the exploits and complaints of Jonah. The Song of Songs was a celebration with laughter and love.

In the prayers of the Orthodox Church the scene at Cana is intimately linked with the scene of Jesus' death:

The Virgin's Lament

The song of Mary's lament on Calvary, is of heart-breaking intensity. Used in the Passion services it set a tone of mourning for the burial of Christ that still liturgically marks the Byzantine Holy Week services for Great Friday:

> As she saw her own lamb being dragged off to slaughter (Isa, 53:7)
> The ewe-lamb Mary followed after, worn out,
> In the company of the other women, crying out:
> Where are you going my child?
> For whose benefit do you run this course so quickly?
> Is it another wedding, as at Cana?
> Is it going there that makes you hurry so
> That you can turn their water to wine once more. ...?

The song develops by depicting Christ on his way to the cross. Counselling his mother not to grieve so broken-heartedly, for his eagerness to deliver the world of suffering beings gives Him a zeal that few can comprehend. The vinegar will be an Astringent which the Physician of life shall use to cure the Wounds of humankind. The spear lances humanity's festering Wounds; the clothes of Christ bandage the suffering body; the cross Serves as a splint and a crutch for the healing of humanity's sicknesses and mortality.

At the Cross the beloved disciple takes Mary to his home. The phrase used in Greek is 'eis ta idia'. Ignace de La Potterie suggests that a translation for this would be that he welcomed her into his intimacy (*Mary: the Mystery of the Church*, pp. 226-228). They became one in spirit – mother and son, servants of the Servant in Spirit. R. E. Browm says that what into his own *(eis ta idia)* is for the beloved disciple is the fact that he is the disciple par excellence. "His own" is the special discipleship Jesus loved. The fact that the mother of Jesus is now the disciple's mother and he has taken her to his own is a symbolic way of describing how one related to Jesus by the flesh (his mother) becomes related to him by the Spirit. (*Death of the Messiah*, p. 1024). The figure of Mary at the foot of the Cross has inspired Christians and many others for generations. The first Marian prayer formed was called "Sub Tuum…".

It goes back to the early centuries of the Church. The text reads: "We fly to thy patronage, O Holy Mother of God, despise not our petition in our necessities, but deliver us from all danger, O ever glorious and blessed Virgin." Christians from a very early age saw their sorrow caught up into Mary's and with her waited for the sorrow to be turned to joy (water into wine). They awaited the words of Jesus. In Tennesse William's play *"A StreetcarNamed Desire"* there is a scene where Blanche has descended into the depths of mental anguish and hell. After the rape by Stanley and the denial by her sister Stella it seems all hope is lost. When Blanche comes on stage in the final scene, she is wearing her red satin robe, suggestive both in colour and tone of Stanley's forced sexual possession of her in the previous scene. As she prepares to leave the house however, she changes her clothes and the colour of her new outfit is specifically remarked upon by the other characters:

Eunice: What a pretty blue jacket.
Stella: It's lilac coloured.
Blanche: You're both mistaken. It's Della Robbia blue. The blue of the robe in the old Madonna pictures.

The broken Blanche sees the Mother of Sorrows with her in her mental anguish. She still has hope that the hell of her isolation will one day be transformed.

Hans Urs Van Balthasar too reflected on Mary and developed a sophisticated theology from Mary's contemplation. In St. Luke we are told how Mary heard many things and pondered them in her heart. (Lk 2: 19, 51). Von Balthasar saw in Mary the style and form of what the church is called to be.

He began with the mysterious text of Jeremiah 31:22 –

"Come home, Virgin of Israel,
come home to these town of yours.
How long will you hesitate (turn here and there)
Disloyal daughter?
For Yahweh is creating something new on earth.
The Woman sets out to find her husband again."

Once unfaithful "Daughter of Sion", "Virgin Israel" will once again seek God, her Spouse and cling to him. Mary is the One who is faithful, she contemplates God, loves Him in her heart and allows Him love her and she becomes a servant of the Servant in bringing others to her Son. This is what Von

199

Balthasar meant by the Marian Principle (or Profile) of the Church. The document of Vatican 11 entitled *Lumen Gentium* describes the Church as the "People of God".

All the people are invited into the presence of the Father in union with Jesus by the Spirit and to live this life where we are called. This aspect of the Church is called the Marian and feminine aspect of the church by Von Balthasar. There are two paragraphs written by Von Balthasar in the 1970s which have since become famous. In the first he speaks of the male principle in the Church so that the Church has

> '... to a large extent put off its mystical characteristics, it has become a Church of permanent conversations, organisations, advisory commissions, congresses, synods, commissions, academics, parties, pressure groups, functions, structures and restructurings, sociological experiments, statistics, that is to say more than ever a male Church, if perhaps one should not say a sexless entity.'

In the second he warns:

> '... Christianity threatens imperceptibly to become inhuman. The Church becomes functionless, soulless, a hectic enterprise without any point of rest, estranged from its true nature by the planner. And because, in this masculine world, all that we have is one ideology replacing another, everything becomes polemical, critical, bitter, humourless and ultimately boring, and people in their masses run away from such a Church.'

> *(Elucidations, pp. 70, 72)*

Some of the examples Von Balthasar sees of the Marian profile are Therese of Lisieux and Abbe Pierre. Therese read St. Paul's hymn to love in 1 Cor 13 and at once she saw her vocation was to be love in the Church. Abbe Pierre (a name given to him in the resistance) at one time trained to be a Capuchin. After the war he formed a community called 'The Emmaus Community'. It was open to anyone from any religion who was broken.

The community was to be a place of acceptance and welcome where the broken ministered to each other. In his encyclical letter on the dignity of women, *Mulieis Dignitatiem*, John Paul 11 cites Von Balthasar (1989) and he cites the term 'Marian Principle of the Church' (A.A. S. 80 (1988). He also speaks of the Marian Profile in his cathecesis on signs of hope in the Church (23rd November, 1998).[1]

The Death of Jesus:

On the Cross Jesus cries out: "I thirst" (*dipso,* 19:28). In the Psalms and Wisdom literature it has a metaphysical meaning. It means to thirst for the springs of salvation, for living water, for the courts of the Lord. The word is found in John, Chapters 4 and 7. The first is in Jesus' conversation with the women of Samaria. "Every one of you who drinks of this water will thirst again, but whoever drinks of the water I shall give him will never thirst again.: (4:13f). The new water of the spirit (the wine of the kingdom) is what Jesus is alluding to. On the last day of the Feast of Tabernacles, Jesus solemnly proclaims his message in the Temple for all to hear: "If anyone thirsts let him come to me and let him drink who believes in me, as the Scripture

---

[1] For a full treatment of the Marian Profile see Brendan Leahy, *The Marian Profile* (London: New City, 2000)

says: From within him shall flow streams of living water."
(7:37f). The Jesus who cries out in need is the one who
gives ever more abundantly.

Thérèse of Lisieux reflected on the words of Jesus, "I thirst"
in poetic form:

> You, the Great God whom all Heaven adores,
> You live in me, my Prisoner night and day.
> Constantly your sweet voice implores me.
> You repeat: "I thirst … I thirst for Love!…"
> I am also your prisoner,
> And I want in turn to repeat
> Your tender, divine prayer:
> "My Beloved, my Brother,
> I thirst for Love! …"
>
> *(P N 31)*

Here Thérèse refers to the mystery of Jesus dwelling in
the soul and his cry for our love. St Francis, in a prayer
attributed to him called the *Absorbeat* , spoke of Jesus
dying for love of our love. The one who asks also gives as
we saw in the story of the Samartian woman. He asked
her for water but offered her much more in return. We too
stand with Therese in need of love and we find ourselves
standing with Mary and the Beloved disciple, hoping to
become that disciple.

When the soldiers hear Jesus' cry "in order to fulfil the
scriptures" (19:28) they raise a sponge full of vinegar, put
on "hyssop" and raised it to his lips (19:29). The Gospel
ties Jesus' words "I am thirsty" to Psalm 69:21 which speaks
of vinegar. "They gave me poison for food and, in my thirst,
gave me vinegar to drink". It also refers to Ps 22:16 which
describes the thirst of the suffering just One – "… my

mouth is dried up like a potsherd and my tongue sticks to my jaws: you lay me in the dust of death." In John 18:11 Jesus says: "Am I not to drink the cup the Father has given me." Jesus wishes to complete the will of his Father. His very food is to do the will of the Father (4:34). The reference to: "hyssop" may also be symbolic. Mark and Matthew refer to a reed on which the bystanders place the sponge full of vinegar (cf. Mk 15:36, Mtt 27:28). Hyssop is ill-suited for the task of holding up a vinegar-soaked sponge since it is leafy and pliant. However, John may intend to evoke the Passover symbolism that has run through the Passion story (cf. B. Lindars, *The Gospel of John*, p. 58, C.K. Barrett, *John,* p. 553). In order to spare the Israelites at the moment of Exodus Moses commanded the elders to " Take a bunch of hyssop, dip it in the blood that is in the basin and touch the lintel and the two doorposts with the blood in the basin. For the Lord will pass through to strike the Egyptian; when he sees the blood on the lintel and on the two doorposts, the Lord will pass over that door and will not allow the destroyer to enter your house to strike you down." (Ex. 12:22f)

The letter to the Hebrews recalls the sprinkling of blood with hyssop that sealed the covenant (9:18-20) in describing Jesus as the mediator of a new covenant forged in the blood of Christ. Jesus is the one who asks but also gives. He says on the cross "It is finished." The verb in Greek comes from the word *teleoithei* which means 'fulfil'. Jesus has fulfilled his mission. R.E. Brown investigates 'it is fulfilled' (teteleisthai) and he sees the answer lying in the previous scene in the formation of the new messianic community of the Mother of Jesus in union with the beloved disciple. (*Death of the Messiah*, p. 1077f). We are called into the community of faith and love. St. Theophane the Recluse described prayer as the descent of the mind into the heart where we find Jesus and in union with him in the Spirit we are in the presence of God. St. Seraphin of Sarov said that the aim of Christian life is to receive the Spirit. In the story of the Passion in John we are on the threshold of the giving of the Spirit. Jesus had said: "The Paraclete, the Holy Spirit, whom the Father will send in my name, he will teach you all things and bring to your remembrance all that I have said to you." (14:26, cf. also 14: 16-17; 15:26; 16:7; 13-14). The spirit clarifies the words of Christ from within, makes them take root so that they may produce fruit for God's people and the whole world.

On the cross we read: "Jesus handed over the Spirit" (cf. De La Patteries' translation, *Hour of Jesus*, p.154, 163f). The word used for spirit here is *pneuma*, the same word that is used for the Holy Spirit. The new community of Mary and the Beloved disciple live in Jesus' Spirit which he has handed over to them. R.E. Brown points out that in 7:37-39 – Jesus promised that when he was glorified those who believed in him would receive the Spirit. This helps explain John's "he gave over [*paradidomai*] the Spirit" (*Death of the Messiah*, 1082). John gave a special place to the beloved disciple in his community and so he introduces a theme here not found in the other Gospels (cf. *Death,* p. 1085). Jesus' work is now complete. The one who asked for love has poured out love.

Origen, a prominent theologian, was born about 80 years after the Gospel was written. For him this moment is essential to understanding the Gospel of John. He writes: "Nobody can really understand the gospel unless one too has reclined on the heart of Jesus and received Mary as mother, as the beloved disciple did." We are called to share that moment, to be the beloved disciple.

Resurrection Appearances:

The first one recorded to have seen Jesus is Mary Magdalene. Jesus appears to her but initially she fails to recognise him but when he calls her name she recognises him.

The appearance to Mary of Magdala:

Meanwhile, Mary stayed outside near the tomb, weeping. Then, still weeping, she stooped to look inside, and saw two angels in white sitting where the body of Jesus had been, one at the head, the other at the feet. They said, "Woman, why are you weeping?" "They have taken my Lord away", she replied "and I don't know where they have put him." As she said this she turned around and saw Jesus standing there, though she did not recognise him. Jesus said, "Woman, why are you weeping? Who are you looking for?" Supposing him to be the gardener, she said, "Sir, if you have taken him away, tell me where you have put him, and I will go and remove him." Jesus said, "Mary!" She know him then and said to him in Hebrew, "Rabbuni!" which means 'Master'. Jesus said to her, "Do not cling to me, because I have not yet ascended to the Father. But go and find the brothers, and tell them: I am ascending to my Father and your Father, to my God and your God." So Mary of Magdala went and told the disciples that she had seen the Lord and that he had said these things to her.

(Jn 20: 11-18)

The friendship is renewed but now at a different level. Jesus' admonition to Mary not to touch him points to the fact that he is now different. He has risen from the dead and his place is at the Father's side.

He shows that the resurrection state is different from the state he was in before he died. He comes and goes mysteriously but in the scene with Thomas he shows that the resurrected one is the one who was crucified.

Appearances to the Disciples:

In the evening of that same day, the first day of the week, the doors were closed in the room where the disciples were, for fear of the Jews. Jesus came and stood among them. He said to them, 'Peace be with you', and showed them his hands and his side. The disciples were filled with joy when they saw the Lord, and he said to them again, 'Peace be with you'.

'As the Father sent me,
so am I sending you.'

After saying this he breathed on them and said:

'Receive the Holy Spirit.
For those whose sins you forgive,
They are forgiven;
For those whose sins you retain,
They are retained.'

Thomas, called the Twin, who was one of the Twelve, was not with them when Jesus came. When the disciples said, 'We have seen the Lord', he answered, 'Unless I see the holes that the nails made in his hands and can put my finger into the holes they made, and unless I can put my hand into his side, I refuse to believe'. Eight days later the disciples were in the house again and Thomas was among them. The doors were closed, but Jesus came in and stood among them. 'Peace be with you', he said. Then he spoke to Thomas, 'Put your finger here; look, here are my hands. Give my your hand; put it into my side. Doubt no longer but believe.' Thomas replied, 'My Lord and my God!' Jesus said to him:

> 'You believe because; you can see me.
> Happy are those who have not seen and yet believe'.

There are many other signs that Jesus worked and the disciples saw, but they are not recorded in this book. These are recorded so that you may believe that Jesus is the Christ, the Son of God, and that believing this you may have life through his name.

(Jn 20: 19-31)

Franciscanism and The Marian Profile:

The saints manifest a new type of conformity to Christ inspired by the Holy Spirit and therefore a new illustration of how the Gospel is to be lived ... a new interpretation of revelation. (Von Balthasar, *Two Sisters*, p. 23ff). In another essay, *Theology and Sanctity*, Von Balthasar speaks of the lives and writings of the holy-ones of God; they can serve as an important theological and spiritual resource. As well as the scientific investigations of scripture the holy ones provide living testimony to the life-giving word of God. All these saints, including Francis and Clare, are examples of the Marian Profile in action – they said 'Yes' to God in the Spirit.

Contemplation and compassion epitomise for me Francis' and Clare's life. This experience included the facing of suffering, the facing of one's human condition in the face of the very mystery of God. Jacopone da Todi (died 1306) was a turbulent Franciscan poet in a turbulent era. Before he became a friar he was anti-church and a cynical lawyer. When his wife Vanna died in an accident he became aware of the hidden penance and prayers she offered for him. She loved him at even deeper levels than he had possibly imagined. This led to his conversion. In one of his lauds, *The Three Stages of Divine Love*, he looks at the demands of compassion:

> When the soul is in harmony with conscience
> It takes joy in the love of its neighbour.
> Then without doubt it is true love,
> Then we can call it charity.

> Love then joins love
> To his suffering brethern;
> And in his compassion he suffers more
> Than the man whose suffering he shares.

> While the brother who was suffering
> Finds respite from his pain,
> The compassionate man suffers anguish,
> Day and night without repose.

> No man can comprehend how this can be
> If the understanding is not infused in him by charity,
> That charity which lies hidden in suffering,
> Waiting to give birth.

As Jacopone suggests, it is compassion that gives access to the other without being intrusive, establishing a real connection with the other by participation in the other's suffering. This way of being human implies vulnerability, availability, solidarity, and empathetic experience of the other. Without providing solutions or answers compassion brings healing and health in that it allows the others to stand in her or his pain and suffering while resisting evil, confusion and surrender, in order to share in the experience of love which is God.

St. Bonaventure was the interpreter of Francis' life and it is through his eyes I look at Francis and the source of his contemplation which overflowed into compassion. Bonaventure maintains that union with Christ brings about a re-creation of the person and his/her relationships.

In the *Legenda Major*, he describes Francis as one who was restored to original innocence because of his intimate relation to Christ. As one conformed to Christ, Francis was drawn into the beauty and order of the world, perceiving creation in its proper relationship to God and experiencing the harmony with creation that the first Adam enjoyed.

Bonaventure writes:

> True piety … drew him up to God through devotion, transformed him into Christ through compassion, attracted him to his neighbour through condescension and symbolically showed a return to the state of original innocence through universal reconciliation with each and every thing.
>
> *(L M 34)*

Bonaventure views ecstatic union as the summit of love between the soul and the crucified Word, drawing one into the glory of the Trinity in union with the Father and the Spirit; this is the mystical passover in Christ. It is love which joins the lover to the beloved and unites them to one another and brings them closer, and which alone can make a soul rise above itself and turn more deeply toward another.

Wayne Hellmann states that the ecstatic contemplation of the transcendent glory of God in the cross transforms one into the compassionate Crucified Christ:

> This "burning love" is the "passion of Christ" in which the soul is transformed into the depths of compassionate love. Seraphic love is compassionate love. It is indeed compassionate love that Bonaventure develops to the fullest. For Bonaventure, Francis' mystical experience of ecstatic contemplation of the transcendent glory of God transforms him into the compassionate crucified Christ. Seraphic glory and the divine intimacy of mystical contemplation not only places one in the seraphic order of angels. It places one on the cross, crucified with Christ.
> *(Wayne Hellman, Bonventuriana 1:355)*

Although Bonaventure affirms union as an ascent to God, ecstatic union with the burning love of the Crucified also draws one out to one's neighbour. It is a love that impels one in the direction of ascent and descent, upward to God and outward to neighbour and world. ... The contemplative who ascends to the glory of God is conformed to the humility of Christ. Whereas in the third degree of love, the soul is conformed to the likeness of God, in the fourth degree she begins to empty herself, taking the form of a servant, following Christ in his passion. In the highest degree of love he states, "the soul goes forth on God's behalf and descends below herself. ... Because of her neighbour.

(cf. Ilia Delio, *Crucified Love*, p. 66f)

Francis, by praying before the crucified, becomes transformed into love and compassion and from that love he reaches out to all as brothers and sisters. He becomes a servant of the Servant, leading others into the peace of God that knows no end. This dynamic of contemplation and compassion leading to transformation describes the religious experience of Clare. She writes to Agnes:

> Gaze upon that mirror each day, O queen and spouse of Jesus Christ, and continually study your face within it, that you may adorn yourself within and without with beautiful robes. ... Instead, blessed poverty, holy humility, and inexpressible charity are reflected in that mirror.

The mirror which Clare invites Agnes to gaze into is the cross of San Damiano, the cross that spoke to Francis and commissioned him to rebuild a dilapidated house. In looking into this image of Christ, Agnes is invited to see her own reflection, as if she were looking at her own mystery. And Clare goes on to suggest that what Agnes will see there is something very familiar.

Look at the border of this mirror, that is the poverty of him who was placed in a manger and wrapped in swaddling clothes. ... Then at the surface of the mirror, consider the holy humility, the blessed poverty, the untold labours and burdens that he endured for the redemption of the whole human race. Then, in the depths of this same mirror, contemplate the ineffable charity that led him to suffer on the wood of the cross and to die there the most shameful kind of death.

What Clare describes here are very ordinary human experiences – birth and poverty; the burdens and labours of life and humility; suffering, shame, death, and charity. These ordinary human experiences are salvific because they were embraced by Jesus.

There is a clear parallel between what Clare invites Agnes to do in looking at the mirror of the cross and what Clare suggests Francis sees when he looks at the Poor Sisters in their life at San Damiano. Both Francis and Agnes are seeing human life. Francis contemplates the life of the Poor Ladies, Agnes is invited to contemplate the life of Jesus Christ in the mirror of the Cross. The juxtaposition of these two texts reveals an important Franciscan insight: Comtemplation is the means for the discovery of the truly human without disguise. The humanity revealed in the fragile, weak flesh of Jesus Christ is the truth of human life. The adjectives which describe the life of Christ reflected in the mirror of the cross, are the same adjectives which describe the life of the Poor Ladies in the mirror of the enclosure of San Damiano. Clare does not stop at this point, however, and continues with an exclamation and exhortation to Agnes:

> Therefore, that mirror, suspended on the wood of the cross, urged those who pass by to consider, saying: "All you who pass by the way, look and see (attendite et videte) if there is any suffering like my suffering." *(Lamentations, 1:12)*
> *(Letter to Agnes of Prague: Armstrong, p. 50-51)*

The model of compassion that Bonaventure presents as a paradigm of Christian discipleship is Mary, the mother of Jesus, and he describes her presence at the scene of the crucifixion as a vicarious martyrdom:

What tongue can tell, what intellect grasp the heavy weight of your desolation, blessed Virgin? You were present at all these events, standing close by and participating in them in every way. This blessed and most holy flesh – which you so chastely conceived ... now torn by the blows of the scourges, now pierced by the points of the thorns, now struck by the reed, now beaten by hands and fists, now pierced by nails and fixed to the wood of the cross ... he looked upon you standing before him and spoke to you these loving words: "Woman, behold your son", in order to console in its trials your soul, which he knew had been more deeply pierced by a sword of compassion than if you had suffered in your own body.

(Lignum Vitae 28)

The significance of Mary at Calvary lies precisely in her role as sharer in the passion of her Son. Physically seeing the external sufferings of Jesus, which are now recapitulated, and experiencing his interior anguish by means of "seeing within", she is a model for all those who desire to participate in mystical death with Christ. We are to be as united to Jesus as Mary was by spiritually giving birth to the Word of God within our soul. Bonaventure illuminates the theme of spiritual motherhood by describing the power of the Holy Spirit within the soul. Giving birth to Jesus in the same way as Mary did, the soul conceives mystically by a gift of grace. Spiritual motherhood is the work of the Spirit in the soul perfected through grace, enabling the soul to become both mother and spouse of the Crucified.

(cf Delio, *Crucified Love*, p. 102f)

Edith Stein was also one in modern time who expressed the same. She was a convert from Judaism and became a Carmelite nun. She was martyred at Auschwitz because her people were originally Jewish. Edith saw something vital happen at the cross. "Mary became our mother beneath the Cross. She loves the souls who follow the Lord right up to beneath the cross. This was the core of Edith's vocation: to carry the cross with Jesus, to stand with Mary on Calvary, to labour for the church.

At the cross, for Edith, 'woman' became 'mother'. Bonaventure describes how Jesus calls us to him to come to experience the transforming love of his Spirit. In the Soliliqiium, he wrote:

Christ on the cross bows his head, waiting for you, that he may kiss you; he stretches out his arms, that he may embrace you; his hands are open, that he may enrich you; his body is spread out, that he may give himself totally; his feet are nailed, that he may stay there; his side is open for you, that he may let you enter there.

Epilogue:

Our prayer journey has been from Rachel's cry to Mary's song. Rachel symbolises suffering humanity which cries out to God. In various times God answered through the prophets and now he has shown his love in Jesus who reveals Him to us. In the Spirit we are called to share in that love. Mary is the one who said "Yes" to God's designs and became Mother of Jesus. When we come to know her son and the God (the Father) he reveals then we can begin to leave Rachel's cry and sing Mary's Song.

I conclude with St. Francis' salutation of the Blessed Virgin Mary. This simple collection of titles forms a litany of greetings describing Mary's role in the plan of salvation. The manuscript tradition suggests a close tie between this piece and the following, the A Salutation of the Virtues, and therefore, presents the Virgin Mary as the model for every Christian who responds to God's virtuous presence in his or her life:

Hail, O Lady,
Holy Queen,
Mary, holy Mother of God,
Who are the Virgin made Church,
Chosen by the most Holy Father in heaven
Whom he consecrated with His most holy beloved Son
And with the Holy Spirit the Paraclete,
In whom there was and is
All fullness of grace and every good.

Hail His Palace!
Hail His Tabernacle!
Hail His Dwelling!
Hail His Robe!
Hail His Servant!
Hail His Mother!

And hail all You holy virtues
Which are poured into the hearts of the faithful
Through the grace and enlightenment of the Holy Spirit,
That from being unbelievers,
You may make them faithful to God.

(*Francis of Assisi, The Saint*, p. 163)

Bibliography:

Anderson, B W,
  -Out of the Depths: The Psalms Speak for us Today
  (Philadelphia, Westminister Press, 1983)

Armstrong, Regis,
  -Francis and Clare (New York, Paulist Press, 1982)
  -Francis of Assisi: The Saint I (London, New
  City Press, 1999)
  -Francis of Assisi: The Founder II, (London
  Navity Press)
  -Francis of Assisi: The Prophet III, (london,
  New City Press 2001)

Ashton, John,
  *-The Identity and Function of the Ioudaioi in the
  Fourth Gospel*, NT 27 (1985)
  -Understanding the Fourth Gospel.
  (Oxford: Clarendon Press, 199)
  -The Interpretation of John. Issues in Religion and
  (Theology 9, London: SPCK, 1986)

Auden, W H,
  -Collected Poems (New York) Vintage Books, 1991

Balentine, Samuel E,
  *-Prayer in the Hebrew Bible: The Drama of
  -Divine-Human Dialogue*
  (OBT, Minneapolis, Fortress Press, 1993)

Barrett, C K,
    -*The Gospel according to St. John.* 2nd ed.
    (London SPCK, 1978)

Beasley, Murray,
    -*John. WBC 36.* (Waco:Word Books, 1987)

Beattie, Tina,
    -*Rediscovering Mary* (London, Triumph, 1995)

Bellow, Saul,
    -*More Die of Heartbreak* (London, Penguin, 1996)

Bernanos, G,
    -*The Diary of a Country Priest*
    (New York/London, Macmillon, 1937)
    -*Letters and Papers from Prison* (London: SCM
    Classics, 2001)

Billman, Kathleen D. and Milgliore, Daniel L.
    -*Rachel's Cry* (Cleveland, United Church Press, 1999)

Bonaventure,
    -*The Soul's Journey into God, The tree of Life,
    The Life of St. Francis.* Translated by Ewert Cousins.
    (New York: Paulist, 1978)

Bonhoeffer, D,
    -*Prayerbook of the Bible* (Minneapolis, Fortress
    Press, 1996)

Bono,
    -Introduction to *Selections from the Book of Psalms*
    (New York, Gnome Press, 1998)

Booth, Wayne,
　　-*A Rhetoric of Irony,* (Chicago University Press, 1974)

Brendan Leahy,
　　-*The Marian Profile* (London: New City, 2000)

Bright, John,
　　-'Jeremiah's Complaints: Liturgy or Expression of
　　Personal Distress' in *Proclamation and Presence*
　　(Eds. John J Durham and JR Porter, London, SCM
　　Press, 1970)

Brown, Raymond E,
　　-*The Death of the Messiah- From Gethesemane
　　to the Grave - A Commentary on the Passion
　　Narratives in the Four Gospels.* 2 vols. (ABRL.
　　Garden City, New York: Doubleday, 1994)

Bruce, F F,
　　-*Philippians* (Peabody, MA, Hendrickson, 1989)

Brueggemann, Walter,
　　-*The Message of the Psalms* (Minneapolis, Augsburg, 1984)
　　-'From Hurt to Joy, From Death to Life' in *The Psalms and
　　the Life of Faith* (Minneapolis, Augsburg Fortress, 1995)
　　-'The Formfulness of Grief' in *The Psalms and the
　　Life of Faith* (Minneapolis, Augsburg Fortress, 1995)
　　-*Isaiah* 40-66 (Louisville, Westminister Press, 1998)
　　-A Shape for Old Testament Theology I - Structure
　　Legetimation - *Catholic Biblical Quarterly* - 47 (1985)
　　-A Shape for Old Testament Theology II - Embrace of
　　Pain - *Catholic Biblical Quarterly* - 47 (1985)
　　-*'Hopeful Imagination'* (Philadelphia Fortress Press 1986)

Buber, Martin,
>*-I and Thou* (New York, Scribner's Sons, 1958)
>*-The Prophetic Faith* (New York, Harper Torchbooks,1960)
>-'The Heart Determines (Psalm 73)' in *On the Bible*
>(New York, Schoken Books, 1968)
>*-Tales of the Hasidim* (New York, Schocken Books, 1991)

Bultmann, Rudolf,
>*-The Gospel of John. A Commentary.*
>(Oxford: Blackwell, 1971)

Cabaud, Jacques
>*-'Simone Weil'* (London Harvill Press, 1964)

Camus, Albert,
>*-The Stranger* (New York, Vintage Books, 1958)
>*-Caligula and Other Plays*
>(New York, Vintage Books, 1958)
>*-The Plague* (London, Penguin, 1960)
>*-The Fall* (London, Penguin Classics, 2000)
>*-The Myth of Sisyphus* (London, Penguin Classics, 2000)
>Chavanes, François,
>*-Albert Camus: Il Faut Vivre Maintenant*
>(Paris, Cerf, 1990)

Cox, D,
>*-The Psalms in the Life of God's People*
>(Slough, St Paul's Publications, 1984)

Crenshaw, J,
>*-A Whirlpool of Torment: Israelite Traditions of*
>*God as an Oppressive Presence*
>(OBT, Philadelphia, Fortress Press, 1984)

Crenshaw, James L,
    -Ecclesiastes (OTL: Philadelphia, Westminister Press, 1987)

Cruickshank, John,
    -Albert Camus and the Literature of Revolt
    (Oxford University Press, 1959)

Crüsemann, Frank,
    -'The Unchangeable World: The Crisis of Wisdom
    in *Koheleth' in God of the Lowly: Socio-Historical
    Interpre tations of the Bible* (Eds.W Schottroff and
    W Stegemann, Maryknoll, Orbis Books, 1979)

Dahood, M,
    -Psalms (3 vols: Anchor Bible 16, 17, 17a) (Gordon
    City, New York, Doubleday, 1966, 1968, 1970)

Davidson, Robert,
    *-The Vitality of Worship: A Commentary on the
    Book of Psalms* (Edinburgh, The Handel Press, 1998)
    *-The Courage to Doubt (*London, SCM, 1983)

Dostoyevsky, Fyodor,
    -The Devils (Harmondsworth: Penguin, 1953)
    -The Brothers Karamazov (Harmondsworth: Penguin, 1958)

Dylan, Bob,
    -'Tomorrow is a Long Time' from *Bob Dylan:
    Lyrics 1962-1985* (London, Paladin, 1987)

Dreyer, Elizabeth A.
    -"Mysticism Tangible Through metaphor" in *The
    Cross in Christian Tradition*, ed. Elizabeth A. Dreyer,
    (New York: Paulist Press, 2000)

Einstein, Albert,
-The World As I See It (London, Bodley Head, 1955)

Fox, Michael V,
A Time to Tear Down and a Time to Build Up
(Cambridge, Eerdman, 1999)

Frankl, Viktor,
-Man's Search for Meaning (New York Pocket Books, 1985)
-The Unconscious God
(New York, Simon & Schuster, 1985)

Fretheim, Terence,
-The Suffering of God
(OBT Philadelphia, Fortress Press, 1984)

Friedman, Maurice,
*-Martin Buber's Life and Work: The Early Years
1878-1923* (New York, EP Dutton, 1981)
- Martin Buder's Life and Work 1945-1965
(Detroit, Wayne State University Press, 1988)

Gaeta, Saverio,
-Il Segreto di Madre Teresa
(Casile Monferrato, Piemme, 2003)

Gebara, Ivone and Maria Clara Bingemar
-Mary, Mother of God, Mother of the Poor
(Maryknoll, Orbis Books, 1987)

Gertsenberger, E S,
-Psalms Part 1 (Grand Rapids, Eerdmans, 1988)
-Psalms Part 2 and Lamentations
(Grand Rapids, Eerdmans 2001)

Gordis, R,
- *The Book of God and Man: A Study of Job*
(University of Chicago Press, 1969)
- *The Book of Job* (New York, Jewish Theological
Seminary of America, 1978)

Gunkel, H,
- *The Psalms: A Form – Critical Introduction*
(Philadelphia, Fortress Press, 1967)

Guttirréz, Gustavo,
- *On Job* (New York, Orbis Books, 1999)

Habel, Norman C,
- *The Book of Job*
(OTL, Philadelphia, Westminister Press, 1985)

Hans Urs Von Balthasar,
- *Elucidations* (San Francisco, Ignatious Press, 1975)
- *Bernanos* (San Francisco, Ignatious Press, 1988)
- *The Glory of the Lord* (7 vols.) (Edinburg: TNT
Clark: 1984-1989)
- *Theodrama* (5vols.) (San Francisco, Ignatious Press,
1988-1995)

Harvey, A E,
- *Renewal Through Suffering* (Edinburg: T.T. Clark, 1996)

Heschel, Abraham J,
- *Man's Quest for God* (New York, Charles Schribner's Sons, 1954)
- *God in Search of Man: A Philosophy of Judaism*
(New York, Farrar, Strauss and Cudahy, 1955)
- 'On Prayer: *Conservative Judaism*', 25, No 1 (Fall, 1970)

Heschel, Abraham J, *(cont.)*
> -*The Prophets* (New York, Jewish Publication Society
> of America, 1962)
> -*Who is Man?* (Stanford University Press, 1965)
> -*The Insecurity of Freedom: Essays on Human Existence*
> (New York, Schocken Books, 1966)
> -'No Religion is an Island' in *No Religion is an Island*
> (Eds. Harold Kasimow and Byron L Sherwin,
> Maryknoll, Orbis Books, 1991)
> -*A Passion for Truth* (Woodstock, Jewish Lights
> Publishing, 1995)

Hopkins, Gerard Manley,
> -*The Works of Gerard Manley Hopkins* (Ware,
> Hertfordshire, Wordsworth Editions, 1994)

Humphries, W Lee,
> *The Tragic Vision and the Old Testament*
> (OBT, Philadelphia, Fortress Press, 1985)

Janzen, J Gerald, *Job:*
> -*Interpretation* (Atlanta, John Knox Press, 1985)

Jinkins, M,
> -*In the House of the Lord* (Collegeville, Liturgical
> Press, 1998)

Jung, C G,
> -*Memories, Dreams, Reflections* (London, Fontana Press, 1995)

Kafka, Franz,
> -*The Trial* (London, Penguin, 1953)

Kazantzakis, Nikos,
   -*Report to Greco*, (Oxford, cassier, 1965)

Kraus, H J,
   -*Theology of the Psalms* (Minneapolis, Augsberg, 1986)

Kübler-Ross, Elizabeth,
   -*On Death and Dying* (New York, Macmillan, 1969)

La Potterie, Ignace de,
   -*Mary in the Mystery of the Convenant.*
   (New York: Alba House, 1992)
   -*The Hour of Jesus. The Passion and resurrection of
   Jesus according to John*: Text and Spirit.
   (St. Paul Publications, 1989)
   -La Parole the Jésus 'Voici ta mère' et l'accueil du
   Disciple (Jn 19, 27b) Marianum 36 (1974)

Larkin, Philip,
   -*Collected Poems* (London, Marvell Press, 1988)

Latourelle, R,
   -*Man and His Problems*, (New york: Alba House, 1985)

Léon,-Dufour, Xavier,
   -*Lecture de l'évangile selon Jean*. 4 Vols. Parole de
   Dieu. Paris: Editions du Seuil, 1988, 1990, 1993, 1996

Lindars, Barnabas,
   -*The Gospel of John*. NCB. (London: Oliphants, 1972)

Marty, M,
   -*A Cry of Absence* (New York, Harper and Row, 1983)

225

Mays, James L,
> -*The Lord Reigns: A Theological Handbook to the
> Psalms* (Louisville John Knox Press, 1994)
> -*Psalms: Interpretation* (Louisville, John Knox Press, 1994)

McCann, J Clinton,
> -*A Theological Introduction to the Book of Psalms:
> The Psalms as Torah* (Nashville, Abingdon Press, 1993)

McCarthy, John and Morrell, Jill,
> -*Some Other Rainbow* (London, Transworld, 1993)

McCuttchon, Stephen P,
> -*Experiencing the Psalms* (Macon, Ga Smyth, Helion, 2000)

Miller, P D,
> -*Interpreting the Psalms* (Philadelphia, Fortress Press, 1986)
> -*They Cried to the Lord: The Form and Theology of
> Biblical Prayer* (Minneapolis, Fortress Press, 1994)

Mitchell, Joni,
> -'The Sire of Sorrow (Job's Sad Song)' from the
> album *Turbulent Indigo* (Regius Records, 1994)
> -'Slouching Towards Bethlehem' and 'God Must be
> a Boogie Man' from the album *Travelogue*
> (Noneush Records, 2002)

Moltmann, Jurgen,
> -*The Crucified God* (London, SCM Press, 1974)

Mowinckel, Sigmund,
> -*The Psalms of Israel's Worship* (Oxford, Oliver
> Blackwell, 1962)

Mumma, Howard,
     -*Albert Camus and the Minister* (Brewster, Mass.,
     Paraclete Press, 2000)

NIB: *New Interpreters' Bible*, (12 vols.) (Nasheville,
     Abingdon Press, 1994-2002)

Nouwen, Henri J M,
     -*The Road to Daybreak*
     (London, Danton, Longman and Todd, 1991)

Peterson, Ingrid J
     -*Clare of Assisi: A Biographical Study* (Quincy III,
     Franciscan Press, 1993)

Pétremant, Simone,
     -*Simone Weil: A Life* (New York, Pantheon Books, 1976)

Rouiller, François,
     -*Le Scandale du Mal et de la Souffrance Chez
     Maurice Zundel* (St-Maurice, Éditions Saint-Augustin, 2002)

Senior, Donald,
     -*The Passion of Jesus in the Gospel of John.*
     (Collegeville: The Liturgical Press, 1991)
     -*The Passion of Jesus in the Gospel of Mark*
     (Wilmington: Glazier, 1984)

Sherwin, Byron, L (Ed.)
     -*No Religion is an Island* (Maryknoll, Orbis Books, 1991)

Soelle, D,
     -*Suffering* (Philadelphia, Fortress Press, 1975)

Solzhenitsyn, A,
>-*Matryona's House and Other Stories* (London,
Penguin, 1971)

Springsted, Eric O,
>-*Simone Weil and the Suffering of Love*
(Cambridge, Cowley Publications, 1986)

St. Francis of Assisi,
>-*Writings and Early Biogaraphies, English Omnibus
of the Sources for the Life of St. Francis.*
Edited by Marion Habig.
(Chicago: Franciscan Herald Press, 1974)

Stockman, Steve,
>-*Walk On: The Spiritual Journey of U2*
(Lake May, Fl. Relevant Books, 2003)

Stokes, Neil,
>-*U2 Into The Heart* (New York: Thunder
Mouth Press, 2003)

Taylor, V,
>-*St. Mark* (London, Macmillan, 1995 ed.)

Telford, W. (ed),
>-*The Interpretation of Mark* (Issues in Religion and
Theology 7; Philadelphia: Fortress, 1985)

Thérèse of Lisieux,
>-*The Poetry of Saint Thérèse of Lisieux*
(Washington, ICS Publications, 2002)

Thompson, Francis,
    -*Collected Poems* (Sevenoaks, Kent, Fisher Press, 1992)

Tillich, Paul,
    -*The Courage to Be* (Yale University Press, 1952)
    -*Systematic Theology - 3 vols* (Chicago University Press, 1971)

Todd, Olivier,
    -*Albert Camus: A Life* (New York, Carroll and
    Graf, 2000)

Van Breemen, Peter G,
    -*As Bread That is Broken*
    (New Jersey, Dimenssion Books, 1974)

Von Balthasar, Hans Urs,
    -*Tragedy Under Grace* (San Francisco, Ignatius Press, 1988)

Waite, Terry,
    - *Taken on Trust* (London, Hodder & Stoughton, 1993)

Weems, Ann,
    -*Psalms of Lament*
    (Louisville, Westminister John Knox Press, 1995)

Weil, Simone,
    -*Waiting For God* (New York, Putman's Sons, 1951)
    -*Intimations of Christianity Among the Ancient
    Greeks* (Boston, Beacon Pres, 1957)
    -*Selected Writings,* 'Modern Spiritual Masters' series
    (New York, Orbis Books, 1998)

Weintraub, Simkay (Ed.),
> -*Healing of Soul, Healing of Body*
> (Woodstock, Jewish Lights Publishing, 1994)

Weiser, Arthur,
> -*The Psalms* (OTL, Philadelphia, Westminister
> Press, 1962)

Westermann, Claus,
> -*Praise and Lament in the Psalms*
> (Atlanta, John Knox Press, 1981)
> -*The Structure of the Book of Job*
> (Philadelphia, Fortress Press, 1981)

Wiesel, Elie,
> -*Night* (New York, Hill and Wang, 1960)

Wilde, Oscar,
> -*Selected Poems*, Edited by Malcolm Hicks
> (Manchester, Carcanet Press Ltd, 1992)

Wink, W. ,
> -*Engaging The Powers* (Menneapolis: Fortress Press, 1992)

Wright, N T,
> -*The New Testament and the People of God*
> (London, SPCK, 1992)

Zundel, Maurice,
> -*Hymne à la Joie* (Quebec, Éditions A Sigier, 1992)
> -*Quel Homme et Quel Dieu?*
> (Saint-Maurice, Éditions Saint-Augustin, 1986)